THE
SANTA FE
COMPENDIUM

WHY WE REALLY *ARE*
"THE CITY DIFFERENT"

THE

SANTA FE
COMPENDIUM

TRIVIA, HISTORY, BESTS, FACTS, OPINIONS,
HUMOR, WHAT TO SEE AND WHAT TO DO

JOHN T. SELF, PhD

To Deb
Thank you for being the drive and the inspiration to accomplish anything

ACKNOWLEDGMENTS:

I'd like to thank Glen Smith for unselfishly sharing his incredible knowledge of Santa Fe, Pen LaFarge for his historical memory and suggestions, and Bryant Rogers for his encyclopedic expertise in all things Native American. Without their help, this book would have been very different, and not in a good way.

Every effort has been made to ensure that the information contained within *The Santa Fe Compendium* is accurate and timely. The author would be pleased to be notified of errors or omissions that would improve future editions.

Please send all comments or suggestions to the author at johnselfauthor@gmail.com

CONTENTS

Chapter 1

GETTING TO KNOW SANTA FE

What Started Us Being "The City Different"?

In the 1920s, Santa Fe officials ordered all buildings in the city to be built with adobe in the Pueblo Indian style. With Victorian, Italian, and Spanish architecture already here, Santa Fe became a true combination of cultures, all helping give Santa Fe its nickname.

But in the beginning.

Since its founding in 1610, Santa Fe has prospered from being the administrative, commercial, and military center. By 1912, however, the city had lost much of its commercial firepower when it suffered a double whammy: in the 1880s, the Atchison Topeka and Santa Fe Railroad bypassed the city in favor of Albuquerque, and Fort Marcy's military reservation closed in the 1890s.

Though Santa Fe maintained its status as a territorial administrative center at the end of the nineteenth century, the city had not prospered. The population had slowly fallen since its peak in 1880, when it had 9,233 people (Census.gov), but by 1910, the census count had dropped to just over 5,000 people. To reverse this decline, Mayor Arthur Seligman wanted Santa Fe to be a tourist destination, so he tasked the Planning Board to produce a comprehensive plan focused on the city's unique architecture, history, and cultural heritage.

The Planning Board produced a unified building code incorporating Santa Fe architectural elements, such as earth-tone colors, flat roofs, rounded edges, vigas, canales, and stucco, that resembled traditional adobe buildings.

The city strictly enforced the code inside the downtown historic district, but used tax credits to encourage the code's adoption outside the district.

The Essentials

- Santa Fe means Holy Faith
- Early Native Americans called Santa Fe the "Dancing Ground of the Sun"
- The early Pueblo people called the Santa Fe area 'Ogapogeh'
- It was nicknamed "The City Different" at the turn of the 20th century.
- Original name: La Villa Real de la Santa Fe de San Francisco de Asis (The Royal Town of the Holy Faith of St. Francis of Assisi)
- Founded by Governor Pedro de Peralta in 1610
- 320+ days of sunshine
- US Geological Survey reports Santa Fe is 7,199 feet above sea level (Denver, Colorado is a mere 5,280 feet above sea level)
- Highest elevation state capital city in the US
- Oldest capital city in US (1610) and 2nd oldest city in the US
- New Mexico became a state in 1912
- Population: 90,639 (2023)
- About 300 art galleries are in Santa Fe
- Capital of New Mexico and the County Seat of Santa Fe County
- % Population over 65 years of age: 24.6% (Census.gov). Sarasota, Florida 37.7%
- % Population over 25 years old with a bachelor's degree or higher: 44.0% (Census.gov) National average is 23.0% (Census.gov)
- Santa Fe is the end of the 800-mile Santa Fe Trail, which started in western Missouri in 1822
- According to Forbes, Santa Fe is the 3rd largest art market in the US (behind New York City and San Francisco)
- Gay-friendly: New Mexico has about 7.4 same-sex couples per 1,000 households, well above the national rate of 5.6, according to the Williams Institute, a research organization based at the University of California-Los Angeles. With this metric, New Mexico ranks No. 6 among states for same-sex couples, trailing only five states concentrated in the Northeast and along the West Coast.

Santa Fe IMPONDERABLES

Why does Santa Fe still have (and want) dirt roads?

Maybe for a couple of reasons. Some roads are still dirt because they are private property, and the owner doesn't want to spend money on paving them. The second, and I suspect the main reason, is that dirt roads are traditional Santa Fe. We like our dirt roads. So there. According to *New Mexico Magazine*, there are still 25,000 miles of unpaved roads in New Mexico.

Why are some Santa Fe traffic lights horizontal and not vertical like every other place?

It might be because the horizontal layout sways less in strong winds. This might be the practical reason, but when the green turn signal is in the center and not at the end, it can be really confusing and dangerous. People tend to turn when they shouldn't and go straight when they shouldn't. You must pay close attention to get it right; inevitably, someone doesn't. After a while, you *do* get used to it, but it is still strange. I suspect the real reason was a sale of defective streetlights that Santa Fe just couldn't resist.

Really?

The League of American Bicyclists has recertified Santa Fe as a Silver-level Bicycle Friendly Community that has been certified since 2011. This is news to all Santa Fe bicycle riders.

Those pesky addresses with 1/2

There are 3 reasons for having fractional house numbers:

1. When new buildings are constructed between two existing buildings, a fractional house number may be assigned to avoid disrupting the existing numbering system that didn't leave space.

2. If a lot is subdivided into two or more smaller parcels, one (or each) of the new lots may be assigned a fractional house number.

3. To accommodate different types of buildings on the same lot. For example, if a house and a commercial unit are located on the same lot, one of them may be assigned a fractional number to distinguish it from the other.

What's the Difference Between Farolito and Luminaria?

Farolito, (farol is Spanish for "lantern") means paper light
Luminaria, ("light" in Spanish) means a small fire or bonfire

Neighborhoods of Santa Fe

- Artist-Hyde Park Road
- Historic Eastside
- Museum Hill
- North Side
- Plaza and Downtown
- Railyard District
- Sierra del Norte
- South Capital

Neighborhoods Out a Little

- Airport Road
- Aldea
- Arroyo Hondo
- Bellamah
- Canoncito
- Casa Solana
- Dos Santos
- Eldorado
- Estancia Primera
- Highway 285 corridor
- La Pradera
- Las Campanas
- Las Dos
- La Tierra and La Tierra Nueva
- Midtown
- Quail Run
- Rancho Viejo
- Rodeo Road
- Santa Fe Summit

- Siler/Rufina
- Sol y Lomas
- Southside
- Tano Road
- Tesuque
- Tierra Contenta
- Zia Vista
- Zocalo

Out more than a little

- Cerrillos
- Galisteo
- Glorieta
- Highway 14 corridor
- Jemez Springs
- La Cienega
- Lamy
- Los Alamos
- Madrid
- Northeast
- Pecos
- Pojoaque
- Rowe
- State Road 599 Corridor

Out too far

- Dallas
- Los Angeles
- New York City
- Paris
- Phoenix

Golf and Country Clubs of Santa Fe

- Black Mesa Golf Club
- Chamisa Hills Country Club
- Chamisa Hills Golf and Country Club
- Cochiti Golf Club
- Marty Sanchez public golf course

- Paako Ridge Golf Club
- Quail Run Club
- Sandia Golf Club
- Santa Fe Country Club & Golf Association
- Tanoan Country Club
- The Club at Las Campanas

Cities/towns/villages in Santa Fe County (population)

- Agua Fria (2,523 in 2022)
- Canada de los Alamos (631 in 2022)
- Cedar Grove (879 in 2021)
- Chimayo (3,208 in 2021)
- Chupadero (285 in 2022)
- Cundiyo (17 in 2020)
- Cuyamungue (479 in 2021)
- Edgewood (6,117 in 2022)
- El Rancho (1,513 in 2022)
- El Valle de Arroyo Seco (1,807 in 2020)
- Eldorado (5,451 in 2023)
- Galisteo (205 in 2021)
- Glorieta (549 in 2022)
- Jaconita (307 in 2021)
- La Cienega (4,110 in 2021)
- La Puebla (1,038 in 2021)
- Lamy (98 in 2023)
- Los Cerrillos (105 in 2023)
- Madrid (270 in 2023)
- Pojoaque (2,457 in 2023)
- Rio Chiquito (211 in 2022)
- Rio en Medio (160 in 2021)
- San Ildefonso Pueblo (675 in 2023)
- San Pedro (88 in 2020)
- Santa Cruz (232 in 2023)
- Santa Fe (89,008 in 2023)
- Sombrillo (105 in 2021)
- Tesuque (1,270 in 2023)

Chapter 2

TRIVIA,
HUMOR,
QUOTES,
AND THE
SMALL STUFF

TRIVIA

New Mexico is the only US state with USA on its license plate.

The Frank Ortiz Dog Park is the largest off-leash dog park in the United States at 138 acres

La Fonda means 'hotel'. So, when you say "the La Fonda Hotel", you're saying the hotel hotel.

The Shed Restaurant has a sister restaurant, La Choza, which, surprise! means The Shed in Spanish.

The Lensic Performing Arts Center's name comes from the names of the owner's grandchildren: Lila, Elias, Nathan, Sara, Irene, and Charles.

New Mexico State University has the Chile Pepper Institute.

Lew Wallace, the former New Mexico Territorial Governor, wrote the novel Ben Hur in 1880 while he was the New Mexico Territorial Governor.

Because we're the "City Different" on New Year's Eve, *nothing* will drop when counting down to midnight.

Acequia Madre means "the mother ditch."

Most unpaved roads in Santa Fe are made of dirt, sand, clay, stone, and caliche. Caliche is a mineral deposit of gravel, sand, and nitrates, which makes for a natural cement.

Zozobra was the inspiration for the Burning Man Festival in California when, in 1986, the creators of Burning Man attended Zozobra in the early 1980s.

Zozobra is Spanish for anguish, anxiety, and gloom.

Since the 1980s, Española has declared itself the Lowrider Capital of the World.

The USS Santa Fe (CL-60) is a Cleveland Class light cruiser that was launched on June 10, 1942, and decommissioned on October 29, 1946. She received 13 battle stars for her wartime service. She had a complement of 1,285 officers and crew.

The USS *Santa Fe* (SSN 763) is a Los Angeles Class attack submarine. Nuclear-powered fast attack submarine, that was launched on December 12, 1992. She is still active and has a complement of 12 officers and 98 crew.

Movies are big in New Mexico, with White Sands being the most filmed location in the state. New Mexico is ranked #8 in the top 10 states for TV and Film productions.

New Mexico is the only US state with an official state question.

The official question of New Mexico: Red or Green (chile sauce)?

The official answer: Christmas (meaning *both* red and green chiles)

In 2007, the Santa Fe River was listed as one of the ten most endangered rivers in the United States

In 1960, the US Postal Service issued a 1 ¼ cent postage stamp honoring the Palace of Governors.

In 1912, New Mexico had only 28 miles of paved road.

According to *New Mexico Magazine*, New Mexico has 25,000 miles of unpaved roads.

The Mother Road (Route 66) is named after John Steinbeck's 1939 book *The Grapes of Wrath*.

Lots of prairie dogs make their home in Santa Fe. Their colonies are called "coteries."

In New Mexico, it is illegal to drink alcoholic drinks in casinos except in casino restaurants.

Will Shuster, the Santa Fe artist who created Zozobra, suffered from mustard gas poisoning during World War I and came to Santa Fe in search of a cure.

New Mexico had the most prisoners of war in WWII. In January 1941, the New Mexico National Guard was called up and sent to the Philippines. In April 1942, the Philippines were captured by the Japanese, including all the New Mexican soldiers. Of the 1,825 New Mexican soldiers, more than half died during capture.

Santa Fe has the highest density of galleries in the US along a half mile of Canyon Road (about 100 galleries)

Why Do We Call the Rainy Season "Monsoon Season"?

Officially, the National Weather Service has designated June 15 - September 30 as monsoon season. The North American Monsoon Systems (NAMS) are continental-scale wind patterns that transport water vapor, causing seasonal rains. They occur when intense summer sunlight causes the land to heat up. The word monsoon comes from the Arabic word 'mausim', meaning weather. Monsoons exist on every continent except Antarctica.

Did You Know?

Street names in Santa Fe County are governed by an ordinance that mandates that any driveway with four or more separate addresses or plots of land must have a street name.

Myth #1

Santa Fe's streets were laid out by letting loose a herd of burros on the plaza and tracking where they went.

There is no definitive answer, but some days, this seems like it could be true.

Myth #2
You must have a passport to visit Santa Fe

False. Santa Fe is in *New* Mexico, not Mexico. However, this does explain why our car tags have the USA on them.

Myth #3
Bill Gates founded Microsoft in a garage in Santa Fe.

False. Bill Gates and Paul Allen were originally in Albuquerque, not Santa Fe. They relocated to Washington State in 1979.

Smoky Bear (AKA Smoky the Bear)

Smokey Bear was a real bear, and Santa Fe played a part. In the Capitan Mountains of New Mexico in 1950, a major wildfire blazed with sightings of a bear cub in a tree trying to get away from the fire. A crew removed the cub from the tree and was found to have bad burns on its paws and hind legs. A New Mexico Department of Game and Fish ranger arranged for the cub to be flown to Santa Fe, where his burns were treated and bandaged. After recovery, the cub went to live at the National Zoo in Washington, D.C., becoming Smokey Bear. He remained at the zoo until he died in 1976. He was buried at his home at the Smokey Bear Historical Park in Capitan, New Mexico.

Santa Fe Dissed

In 1926, Route 66 went through Santa Fe, but there were serious engineering challenges from Albuquerque to Santa Fe, including a 2,000-foot elevation change, hard land, and many sharp turns. Back then, road construction was not done with machinery but with animals and humans. In 1937, the US government bypassed Santa Fe, saving 107 miles of construction and driving but saying goodbye to Santa Fe.

Bad Albuquerque Behavior

When it became apparent that Santa Fe would be the capital and not Albuquerque, Albuquerque officials lobbied to have the railroad bypass Santa Fe.

They were successful, causing Santa Fe's economy to decline, while Albuquerque's economy grew because it had a railroad depot.

HUMOR

How can you tell when people are from Santa Fe?
Santa Feans walk on the street even when there are sidewalks.

A Texas couple is heading towards Santa Fe
and see a sign that says "Pojoaque."
They start discussing how the word is supposed to be pronounced,
which turns into an argument.
"It must be PoJo-Q!"
"No, PoJOA-kwee!"
Eventually, they decide to ask someone, so they exit, stop at the first place
they find, and walk up to the counter.
"Look, we're arguing about the name of this place. Do you mind telling us
how to pronounce it, and say it nice and slow so we get it right?"
The guy at the counter looks at them and then slowly says, "…LOT. A.
BURG. ER."

Why is it called tourist season if we can't shoot at 'em?

JUST ONE GROANER (with apologies)

Why didn't the three hombres not cross the road?
Because the sign said, 'No Tres Passing'.

QUOTES

- The best pick-up line in Santa Fe:
  "Hello, I'm Ben. I've got water rights."

- "The art world needs to get shaken up a little bit." Quote from Meow Wolf's movie, "Our Story." www.Meowwolf.com/about

- When the Santa Fe Opera burned down in 1969, and the only thing remaining was a staircase, one person commented that it was a staircase to nowhere. But when John Crosby, the founder of the Santa Fe Opera, saw it, he said it was the "staircase to the future."

- "Occasionally, we find an invited guest is insane. This generally cheers us all up. We know we're on the right track". Cormac McCarthy writing about SFI (Santa Fe Institute)

- "One tequila, two tequila, three tequila, floor." Anonymous

- "There are more writers in Santa Fe per capita than any other place in the United States", anonymous and unsubstantiated (you know who you are)

- "It's the only place in the world where you can wear a cowboy hat and Birkenstocks and not look out of place. I have both." Alan Arkin

- "Every calculation based on experience elsewhere fails in New Mexico", Lew Wallace, former New Mexico Territorial Governor.

- "Poor New Mexico. So far from God and so close to Texas." Maybe Manuel Armijo, Governor of New Mexico under the Mexican Republic, but it was probably a take-off of "Poor Mexico. So far from God and so close to the United States" attributed to Porfirio Díaz, President of Mexico.

- "You look inside. You experiment. You explore. You do things that are different", Alan Houser, sculptor.

- "Santa Fe: The most wonderful 50-mile square in America" Santa Fe Chamber of Commerce Circa 1924.

- "We are not spectators; all human landscape is not a work of art." John Brinckerhoff Jackson, landscape architect, and writer.

- "We should have another war with Old Mexico to make her take back New Mexico." Susan Wallace in a message to her son on her unhappiness living in Santa Fe in 1879. Susan Wallace was the author of *The Land of the Pueblos* and wife of Lew Wallace, the Governor of New Mexico Territory. Another quote by Susan Wallace on the pleasures of riding the train: "Oh! The horror of the chamber of torture known to the hapless victims as the sleeping car."

- "God and the Great Spirit gave me [hands] that work. God gave me that hand, but not for myself, for all my people." Maria Martinez, potter, San Ildefonso Pueblo

- "No one in Santa Fe cares what you do, as long as you tell me." Unknown

- When Santa Fe author and historian Fray Angélico was asked whether the little lights should be called farolito or luminaria, he replied, "Whatever."

- "I wanted to live in this city, which is this incredible collection of completely disparate backgrounds, educations, skin colors, and music." Ali McGraw in an interview with *Santa Fe Magazine.*

- They said, "Why don't you move to Taos?" and I said, "What the hell is Taos?" Ned Bittinger, portrait painter

- "This higher standard [of professionalism] is neither a matter of ethics nor a matter of malpractice. It is a standard that we ought to aspire to as a matter of life-long commitment. It is a journey without hope of official reward or fear of official sanction. We are looking for a better way…doing right for right's sake." Pamela B. Minzer, the first female Chief Justice of the New Mexico Supreme Court

- "Often, people think about Native Americans as we were envisioned at the turn of the century. If we're not walking around in buckskin and fringe, mimicking the stereotype in dress and art form, we're not seen as real. Native Americans are here, and we are contemporary people, yet we are very much informed and connected to our history." Charlene Teters, Native American artist and activist.

↵ "Do you suppose it's our altitude?"
"Nope, it's *their* latitude." Anonymous

↵ "To create one's world in any of the arts takes courage." Georgia O'Keeffe

↵ "This town is not for sale. It belongs to the community." Debby Jamarillo, Mayor of Santa Fe

↵ "If the army placed the Navajo on a reservation far from the haunts and hills and hiding places of their country, they would acquire new habits, new ideas, new modes of life. Civilizing the Navajo could be best achieved through their children: The young ones will take their places without these longings: and thus, little by little, they will become a happy contented people." James Carleton to Thompson, September 19, 1863, in *Navajo Roundup: Selected Correspondence of Kit Carson's Expedition against the Navajo*, 1863–1865, ed. Lawrence C. Kelly (Boulder, CO: Pruett Publishing, 1970), 56–57.

Chapter 3

EXPLORING
SANTA FE

EXPLORING
Off and On
the Beaten Path

109 East Palace: You'll miss this plaque if you're not *really* trying to find it. From 1943 to 1945, this was an important address since everyone, including scientists, working on the atomic bomb with the Manhattan Project at Los Alamos started here. It stayed active until it closed in 1963. Now, only a smallish plaque in the back of the gallery commemorates this place. An excellent book by the same name was published by Jennet Conant.

Acequia Madre House is a historic residence built in 1926 in the Territorial Revival style. It was constructed by three amazing women: Eva Scott Fényes, her daughter Leonora Scott Muse Curtin, and her granddaughter Leonora Frances Curtin Paloheimo. It spans over 150 years of family history. The Acequia Madre House houses extensive collections including:

1. Artwork: Several hundred paintings and prints, including works by artists such as Awa Tsireh, Julian Martinez, Muhammad Ben Ali Ribati, and many others.

2. Pottery: A worldwide pottery collection featuring pieces by Maria Martinez, Margaret Tafoya, Arabia, and sculptor Frank Applegate.

3. Traditional Arts and Crafts: The family supported local traditions by founding the Spanish Colonial Arts Society in 1925 and establishing the Native Market in Santa Fe, Tucson, and New York.

4. Photographs: Over 6,000 photographs are available online in the New Mexican Digital Collections of the University of New Mexico.

The Acequia Madre House is a place where women's achievements and contributions are celebrated and a perfect fit for the Women's International Study Center. It sits on three acres in the historic section of Santa Fe and includes a caretaker cottage, gardens, and grounds. 614 Acequia Madre.

Big Dog Swing. 362 Grant Avenue. This large metal dog is 12 feet tall and 20 feet long, with a porch swing under its belly. It was made by artist Don Kennell in 2011.

Burro Alley. It got its name honestly because Burros carried firewood to sell in Burro Alley. Here, you'll find a beautiful life-size bronze sculpture of a wood-carrying burro, sculpted by Charles Southard in 1988.

Cars and Coffee. Come out to see hundreds of cars, from Ferraris to Corvairs. It's very social; every owner loves to talk about their car. This takes place on the first Saturday of each month, from 9:00 to 11:00 a.m., in the huge parking lot next to Kakawa Chocolate, 1050 Paseo De Peralta.

The Dennis O'Leary Tombstone can be found at the Santa Fe National Cemetery. Pvt. O'Leary (1877-1901) entered the military but was miserable and never fit in. There are two versions of what happened next:

The first version: Private O'Leary went AWOL from Fort Wingate (near Gallup). He was gone for several weeks, and when he showed up without an excuse, he was court-martialed and sentenced to military jail. After he got out, he committed suicide. He left a suicide note saying he had left a "memento" in the mountains, gave directions, and suggested taking a team of horses and a wagon to retrieve the "memento." When the soldiers got there, they found a large sandstone tombstone carved figure of an almost-life-size soldier reclining against a tree trunk wearing boots and a cartridge belt. Behind the trunk was the inscription: "Dennis O'Leary Pvt., Co. I, 23 Infty, died Apr. 1, 1901, age 23 yrs & 9 mo." During his weeks away from Fort Wingate, Pvt. O'Leary had carved his own tombstone and inscribed the date of his death.

The second version: When Private O'Leary died, a friend of O'Leary's became so disconsolate that he deserted the Army and went into the hills to carve the tombstone. When he returned, he requested permission to go back into the hills with some men and a wagon to bring the carving back. Even though he had gone AWOL, the commanding officer was so touched by the friendship that his only punishment was to carve a base for the monument.

Private O'Leary was buried at Fort Wingate, but when the fort closed, everyone, including Pvt. O'Leary, was reburied in the Santa Fe National Cemetery, 501 N Guadalupe St.

Doodlet's is a unique toy store with 140,000 different items. 120 Don Gaspar.

Double Take is a fun place to wander that is full of western-themed consignment goods from boots to furniture. Open Wed – Sat 11:00 am-5:00 pm, Sun 12:30 to 4:30 pm. 320 Aztec Street

El Rancho de Las Golondrinas (Ranch of the Swallows) is scheduled to reopen to the public sometime in 2024. The ranch is located on 200 acres just south of Santa Fe. The museum opened in 1972 as a living history museum dedicated to the history, heritage, and culture of 18th and 19th-century New Mexico. Original buildings on the site date from the early 1700s. www.golondrinas.org

Ethyl the Whale is an 82-foot-long sculpture made from recycled plastic. It holds the Guinness Book of World Records for the largest recycled sculpture. According to one of its sculptors, Yustina Salnikova, the idea behind Ethyl was that every 9 minutes, the weight of a blue whale in plastic is dumped into the ocean. In 2019, Meow Wolf purchased Ethyl, disassembled it, and moved it to its present location. The address, 86 College Dr, appears to be only a suggestion; Look for it on the loop around the back end of Santa Fe Community College.

Five and Dime General Store on the Plaza is like stepping back in time. Here, you'll find almost everything, including the best Frito Pie. Before it was a Five and Dime, it was a Woolworth's which is where the very first Frito pie was created by Teresa Hernández, who made them in the Frito bags as complete lunches for workers.

Labyrinth at the Cathedral Basilica St. Francis of Assisi. You'll find a plaque explaining that the labyrinth was added in 2003 as part of the cathedral's landscape remodel. The design is a replica of one built around the year 1200 in the nave of a cathedral in Chartres, France. The plaque states: "The labyrinth's path is like the path of life; there are twists and turns, feelings of being lost, encounters with others on your path, the thrill of accomplishment at the center, and sometimes a flash of insight before returning." For more information on labyrinths, check out the Santa Fe based "The Labyrinth Resource Group" at **https://labyrinthresourcegroup.org/home/**

La Conquistadora, Our Lady of Conquering Love is a 30-inch-tall wooden statue of the Virgin Mary, found in the Lady Chapel of the Cathedral Basilica of St. Francis of Assisi. She was made between 1448 and 1648 and is believed to be the oldest continuously venerated Virgin Mary likeness in the United States. 131 Cathedral Pl.

M and M Dinosaurs is a life-size brontosaurus family of three. It is drive-by only and just a bit (a lot) quirky. M and M Garage Doors owns it. 246 Dinosaur Trail.

Meow Wolf. If you've not experienced Meow Wolf, you should. It is part Disney Land, part immersive art explosions, and part, well, you'll just have to go. But it is all fun, interesting, and very, very different. For all ages. There are many Meow Wolfs now, but this one is the first, and Meow Wolf is headquartered here: 1352 Rufina Circle.

The Miraculous Staircase of Loretto Chapel can be found in the Loretto Chapel. The Loretto Chapel itself was built in 1878. An anonymous carpenter built the staircase with two 360-degree turns with no visible means of support. The staircase has been featured in TV specials and movies, including "Unsolved Mysteries" and the full-length movie *The Staircase*, starring William Petersen and Barbara Hershey. 207 Old Santa Fe Trail.

Museum Hill is a compact area that includes the Museum of Spanish Colonial Art, The Museum of International Folk Art, The Museum of Indian Arts and Culture, The Wheelwright Museum of the American Indian, and The Santa Fe Botanical Garden. While you're there, walk over to the perfectly named restaurant, the Museum Hill Café, located at 710 Camino Lejo.

The Museum of International Folk Art, Girard holds the largest collection of international folk art in the world with over 130,000 objects from all over the world. 706 Camino Lejo on Museum Hill.

The New Mexico Capitol Art Collection is inside the State Capitol Roundhouse. It is a permanent, public collection of contemporary art by New Mexico artists. It has been said that this art collection is the best-kept secret in Santa Fe. In other words, it is well worth the visit. 415 Don Gaspar Ave.

The New Mexico Penitentiary, AKA "The Old Main," is where the most brutal prison riot in US history took place in 1980. Walking tours are available. Scary stuff. 4311 NM-14.

The Railyard has become a destination all its own. It's a happening area that is great to explore with restaurants, art galleries, shops, and a movie theater. The Railyard is home to the Santa Fe Farmers Market as well as the Artisan Market (Sundays 10:00 am – 3:00 pm). Oh, there really is a railyard. It is used by the RailRunner as well as Sky Railway, which offers a range of excursions. https://railyardsantafe.com/

The **Railyard Farmer's Market** is the largest in the state and is open year-round. It is also home to the Railyard Artisan Market, which features jewelry, musical instruments, pottery, and much more. All items are made by New Mexico artisans. Open Saturdays (8:00 am to 1:00 pm and Wednesdays during summer).

Rio Grande Cutthroat Trout is in front of the Santa Fe Convention Center. You'll see 27 granite pieces (24"h x 18"w x 48"d) swimming. Why cutthroat trout, you ask? Because the Cutthroat trout is the state fish. But you knew that—at least *now* you know that.

Santa Fe Children's Museum is a hands-on kids' museum that features a climbing wall, a garden & a puppet stage, plus interactive classes. Closed Monday and Tuesday. 1050 Old Pecos Trail.

Santa Fe National Cemetery is open daily from sunrise to sunset. It has over 68,000 buried there, including Tony Hillerman and Oliver LaFarge plus many Congressional Medal of Honor winners.

Santa Fe Opera backstage tours are offered during June, July, and August. They are available Monday through Saturday at 9:00 a.m. and last about 45 minutes. Adult tickets are $10, and anyone 6 to 22 years of age is free. Reservations are encouraged.

Scottish Rite Temple was completed in 1912. It is available for limited, exclusive rentals for weddings, concerts, fundraisers, or other special occasions. The temple also supports numerous non-profit community organizations. It was one of the film locations for the 2016 film Whiskey Tango Foxtrot. Tours are available on Tuesdays and Thursdays from 10:00 a.m. to 2:00 p.m. 463 Paseo De Peralta.

SITE Santa Fe presents three to four exhibitions, dozens of unique public programs, and a range of programs for young people each year. It presents artists from around the world while also supporting locally based artists with career development opportunities and significant exhibition opportunities. Admission is free. It is closed on Tuesday and Wednesday. 1606 Paseo de Peralta. (https://sitesantafe.org/)

St. Francis Cathedral (The Cathedral Basilica of St. Francis of Assisi) was built by Archbishop Jean Baptiste Lamy between 1869 and 1886 on the site of an older adobe church, La Parroquia, which was built in 1714–1717. It is open to visitors Tuesday through Friday from 9:30 a.m. to 4:00 p.m. and Saturdays from 9:30 a.m. to 3:00 p.m. 131 Cathedral Place.

Ten Thousand Waves is an exceptional high-end spa, restaurant, and hotel. 21 Ten Thousand Waves Way.

Tesuque Glassworks is a fun place to look around, see glass being blown, and browse the many glass pieces to buy. 1510 Bishops Lodge Rd.

Tesuque Village Market (8 miles) is a quirky, rustic restaurant, bar, and general store that serves breakfast, lunch, dinner, and drinks. 138 Tesuque Village Rd.

Best Day Trips Less Than 3 hours of Driving Time

1. **Diablo Canyon** (13 miles): **Why?** It's a great hike with great views, beautiful scenery everywhere, unique rock formations, interesting geology (basalt and sedimentary), and flora and fauna.

2. **Poeh Cultural Center** (15 miles): **Why?** It is dedicated to preserving and revitalizing the cultural heritage of the Tewa-speaking Pueblos of northern New Mexico. It serves as a gathering place for the respectful sustaining of Tewa traditions through being, doing, and sharing. European contact in the 16th century systematically stripped the Pueblo of Pojoaque of its culture and traditions. The Poeh Cultural Center revitalizes and sustains these cultural traditions, emphasizing the arts and cultures of all Pueblo People. The center's facility resembles a traditional Pueblo village, complete with adjacent art studio buildings and outdoor gathering areas. Visitors can explore rotating galleries, a permanent pueblo history exhibition, outdoor sculptures, a theater space, and a native arts gift shop. The Poeh Cultural Center also hosts dialogues, workshops, and educational programs, fostering cultural exchange and understanding.

3. **Bandelier National Monument** (21 miles): **Why?** It is one of the National Park Service's oldest since it was established the same year that the National Park Service itself started in 1916. It is known for its architectural sites but also includes 23,000 acres of wilderness and over 70 miles of trails from easy (1.2-mile main loop trail) to challenging. You can even climb ladders into several of the carved rooms called 'caveats' ranging from easy to challenging, like Alcove House, which requires four ladders and a 140-foot climb.

4. **Cerrillos**, the town, not the road (23 miles): **Why?** Interesting town to explore with the Black Bird Saloon, Mary's Bar, Casa Grande Trading Post, Mining Museum and Petting Zoo, and art galleries. Several movies were filmed here, including *Young Guns, Outrageous Fortune, We're the Millers,* and *Nine Lives of Elfego Baca.*

5. **Chimayo** (23 miles): **Why?** It is known for the El Santuario De Chimayo, where its dirt floor is said to have healing powers. Be forewarned: During Easter weekend, tens of thousands of pilgrims travel from Santa Fe to Chimayo. It is also known for the weavings of the Ortega and Trujillo families, and you can visit Centinela Traditional Weaving Arts and Ortega's Weaving. A good place to stop for lunch is at Rancho de Chimayo.

6. **Madrid** (23 miles) **Why?** Really interesting old mining town that feels like you've stepped back in time. In its day, it was a center of hippie counterculture. It is a great place to wander, have a meal at rustic restaurants, and browse stores. The movie, *Wild Hogs* was filmed here.

7. **New Mexico Wildlife Center (NMWC)** (24 miles): **Why?** This was founded in 1986 by local veterinarian Dr. Kathleen Ramsay. It was originally formed as a rehabilitation center for injured birds, but the organization evolved to treat all New Mexico wildlife. The center is open for visitors Tuesday-Sunday from 9:00 am to 4:00 pm., located at 19 Wheat Street, in Espanola.

8. **Los Alamos** (26 miles): **Why?** There are two outstanding museums: The Bradbury Science Museum, all about the Manhattan Project and the development and creation of the atomic bomb, and The Los Alamos History Museum, which ranges from the Pueblo People to the Manhattan Project, including the Oppenheimer House and a guest cottage where General Groves stayed. Los Alamos started as the Los Alamos Ranch School, which taught basic ranching and outdoor survival skills to young men. During WWII, Los Alamos was known by its code name "Site Y" by military personnel and "The Hill" by locals. Los Alamos was essentially closed during WWII, accessible only by two gates. Today, the population of Los Alamos is around 13,000, with a high school graduation rate of 93.3%. According to Kiplinger, it has the highest concentration of millionaires in any US city, with 13.2% of households being mil-

lionaires and the highest percentage of doctoral degrees in the nation, with 6.9% of people older than 25 having doctorate degrees.

9. **Pecos National Historical Park** (27 miles): **Why?** It has ancient Pueblo ruins dating back over 12,000 years. You'll see evidence of Spanish colonization, including missions and other historical structures. It is the site of the Battle of Glorieta Pass, the Westernmost Civil War battle. It is huge, covering 5,000 acres.

10. **Valles Caldera National Preserve** (37 miles): **Why?** Over a million years ago, a volcano erupted and then collapsed, creating a 13-mile circular depression called a caldera. When you consider how big and powerful a 13-mile-wide volcano would be, it is breathtaking and humbling. The National Park Service states that the caldera is dormant, but not extinct, which is why it sometimes shows signs of volcanic life with hot springs and boiling sulfuric acid fumaroles (vents or openings) where volcanic gases and vapors are emitted. The Valles Caldera is on land that has streams, forests, and meadows which is very different from New Mexico's usual brown, dry landscape. The caldera is up at 9,000 feet elevation, so the views are incredible. There's elk and other wildlife, really (really) dark night skies, winter skiing, excellent hunting and fishing, and rural quiet, making the caldera great to visit year round.

11. **Puye Cliff Dwellings** (38 miles): **Why?** To see cliff & cave dwellings, early Pueblo architecture, an original Harvey House, and stunning views of the valley. Open Thursday through Monday, closed Tuesdays, and Wednesdays. Tours start at 8:30 am every half hour.

12. **Tent Rocks National Monument** (39 miles): **Why?** The incredibly cone-shaped tent rock formations are the products of volcanic eruptions that occurred 6 to 7 million years ago and left pumice, ash, and tuff deposits over 1,000 feet thick. There is a national recreation trail that ranges from 5,570 feet to 6,760 feet above sea level and is for foot travel only providing hiking, birdwatching, geologic observation, and plant identification. While uniform in shape, the tent rock formations vary in height from a few feet up to 90 feet. Unfortunately, dogs are not allowed in the Monument.

13. **Jemez Springs** (Pronounced HAY Maze) (44 miles): **Why?** Jemez Springs became a tourist destination way back in the 1800s because of

its natural mineral hot springs. You can hike to Spence Hot Springs near Soda Dam or McCauley Hot Springs, near Battleship Rock in the Santa Fe National Forest. If you're not into working for your hot springs fix, there are many commercial hot springs, spas, and bathhouses in Jemez Springs.

14. **Ojo Caliente Hot Springs** (44 miles): **Why?** Two words: Hot springs. When it opened in 1868, it was the country's first health resort. Each of the 7 hot spring pools is naturally sulfur-free and rich in iron, arsenic, soda, and lithia. The village of Ojo Caliente is nearby.

15. **Abiquiu** (49 miles): **Why?** It is most famous for being the home of Georgia O'Keeffe, who lived there from 1949 until shortly before she died in 1986 at 98 years of age. The O'Keeffe Home and Studio is now a popular museum, and Ghost Ranch, where she once lived, is a multipurpose destination with event rentals, camping, and more. Make sure you call for reservations in advance to see the O'Keeffe Home and Studio. Abiquiu is also a very popular film location for Westerns and other movies including the opening scene of *Indiana Jones and the Kingdom of the Crystal Skull, Cowboys & Aliens, City Slickers, Red Dawn, Wyatt Earp, The Last Outlaw,* and the TV series *Earth 2.*

16. **Albuquerque International Balloon Fiesta** (50 miles): **Why?** The Albuquerque International Balloon Fiesta is now the largest balloon event in the world. Held each year during the first week of October, it features about 600 balloons and 700 pilots.

17. **Ghost Ranch** (55 miles): **Why?** Ghost Ranch is a 21,000-acre retreat and education center located close to the village of Abiquiu. It was the home and studio of Georgia O'Keeffe, as well as the subject of many of her paintings. Ghost Ranch is also known for its concentration of fossils, the most famous being the theropod dinosaur Coelophysis. Many movies have been filmed here, such as *Red Dawn* (1984), *City Slickers* (1991), *No Country for Old Men* (2007), *Cowboys and Aliens* (2011), *The Lone Ranger* (2013), *The Ballad of Buster Scruggs* (2018), and *Oppenheimer* (2023).

18. **Albuquerque** (58 miles): **Why?** The Old Town is great for walking around, with more than 150 locally owned and operated businesses. It's worth the trip to eat at the Los Poblanos Historic Inn and Organic Farm for their restaurant, Campo, and a visit to their store, The Farm Shop. There's also a branch of their retail store, Farm Shop Norte and Bar Norte

in Santa Fe. Albuquerque also has a "Breaking Bad" tour. If you don't want to drive, take the Rail Runner from Santa Fe and enjoy the ride.

19. **Earthship Biotecture, 2 Earthship Way, Taos** (58 miles): **Why?** This is an interesting, but very brief visit, probably a side trip from Taos. Stop at the Earthship Visitor Center to learn all about sustainable architecture and living. Self-guided tours last about 10 minutes and are available 7 days a week with guided tours available Thursday-Sunday from 3-4:30 pm. You can rent one of the model homes at the Greater World Community for the night and experience off-grid life in luxury (2 nights minimum).

20. **Sandia Peak Tramway** (59 miles): **Why?** It's a 2.7-mile tramway traveling up to the 10,378-foot crest of the Sandia Mountains allowing views of 11,000 square miles. At the top, you can eat at the TEN 3 Restaurant (get it?) for a dining experience with incredible views.

21. **Las Vegas** (70 miles): **Why?** Founded in 1835, Las Vegas is the Old West personified and is a popular movie location for Western movies. Stop by the visitor Center for a free map that guides you to historic places and landmarks. Don't miss the City of Las Vegas Museum & Rough Rider Memorial Collection. Why is the Rough Rider Memorial Collection in Las Vegas? Las Vegas was the home to the Rough Rider Reunion for years. Why were the reunions there? Great question. 727 Grand Avenue. The museum is open from 10:00 am to 4:00 pm on Tuesday-Saturday and closed on Sunday, Monday, and city holidays. No charge for admission, but a $2 per donation is suggested. Bonus: It has the only classic drive-in left in New Mexico.

22. **Kit Carson Park, 211 Paseo Del Pueblo Norte, Taos** (72 miles): **Why?** The main reason for going to this park is that the man himself, Kit Carson, is buried in the 150-year-old Kit Carson Cemetery. It also offers a ¾ mile walking track.

23. **The Love Apple restaurant, Taos** (73 miles): **Why?** The name! Such a great name. Intimate, cozy, and relaxing atmosphere with usually excellent service. Open Wednesday-Sunday, 5:00 pm-9:00 pm. Note: Bring cash, as they don't take credit cards.

24. **Rio Grande Gorge Bridge** (80 miles): **Why?** At 650 feet above the river, it is the second-highest bridge on the U.S. Highway System and the fifth-highest bridge in the United States. There's also a nice hiking trail along the edge of the gorge.

25. **Chama** (106 miles): **Why?** It has an even higher elevation than Santa Fe at 7,860 feet. Take a day trip from Chama on the historic Cumbres & Toltec Scenic Railroad steam trains which leave the Chama depot daily from Memorial Day weekend to mid-October. Chama has been featured in several films, including *The Good Guys and the Bad Guys* (1969) *The Cowboys* (1972), *Bite the Bullet* (1975), *The Ballad of Gregorio Cortez* (1982), *Butch and Sundance: The Early Days* (1989), *Indiana Jones and the Last Crusade* (1989), *Wyatt Earp* (1994), *Wild Wild West* (1999), *All the Pretty Horses*, (2000), *Appaloosa* (2008), *A Million Ways to Die in the West* (2014), *Godless* (2016), and *Hostiles* (2017). Three members of the Unser family, Al Unser Sr., Bobby Unser, and Al Unser Jr., famous for winning the Indianapolis 500 nine times, have owned or still own ranches in Chama.

26. **Sky City Cultural Center and Haak'u Museum, In the Pueblo of Acoma** (108 miles): **Why?** It is the oldest continuously inhabited settlement in North America and just the 28th Historic Site designated by the National Trust for Historic Preservation. This 500-year-old Indian village sits atop a tall rock formation still inhabited by the Acoma. You can meet the Native American artisans who create handcrafted jewelry, pottery, and other crafts. It's a very good gift shop, too!

27. **Sky Railway** (2 to 3 hours): **Why?** Ride the rails with lots of choices of themes including Wine, Beer, Margarita, Murder Mystery, Jazz, Flamenco, Stargazing, Sunset, and others, all with live music. Fares from $109 to $139. The rail excursions all start and return to the Santa Fe Depot located at 430 West Manhattan.

A Little Longer Than 3 Hours

1. **Rail Runner** (1.5 hours each way): **Why?** Because trains are fun and an easy way to visit Albuquerque. Get on at the Santa Fe Depot located at 430 West Manhattan.

2. **Taos and the High Road** (55 miles each way): **Why?** The High Road is the more scenic route to Taos, going through Nambe and Chamaya taking about 30 minutes longer at 2 hours than the Low Road, which takes about 1.5 hours.

3. **Chama** (108 miles): Take the Cumbres and Totec scenic railroad.

4. **Pie Town** (157 miles): **Why?** It's the town that pie built with a population of around 120. The Pie-O-Neer Homestead Café is located at 5613 US-60 or as the locals call it, Pie 60.

5. **Very Large Array (VLA)** (170 miles): **Why?** The Visitor Center features an award-winning documentary narrated by Jodie Foster plus exhibits describing radio astronomy and the VLA telescope. A self-guided walking tour takes you to the base of one of the giant dish antennas. The VLA was placed here because the mountains provide shelter from the radio frequency transmissions of Albuquerque. The VLA is made up of 27 parabolic dishes that are 82 feet in diameter and can be independently moved by a transporter along rails laid out in an enormous Y pattern. A gift shop offers VLA souvenirs and educational materials.

6. **Trinity Site** (about 190 miles): **Why?** On July 9, 1945, the first atomic bomb was detonated in the White Sands Missile Range, about 60 miles north of the White Sands National Park. In 1965, a monument was erected there, called Ground Zero. In 1975, the National Park Service designated Trinity Site as a National Historic Landmark, which includes the base camp, where the scientists and support group lived; the McDonald ranch house, where the plutonium core was assembled; and of course, Ground Zero. Visits to the site are only allowed on the first Saturday in April and the third Saturday in October. The rest of the year the site is closed to the public because it lies within the impact zone for missiles fired into the northern part of White Sands Missile Range. No argument here.

7. **Chloride, NM** (190 miles): **Why?** It started in 1880 when silver ore was discovered. This just might be a ghost town, but today, it does have a population of around 20. Among the many mines near Chloride, the St. Cloud mine is still in operation, but not for silver. The Pioneer Store is a museum with a gift shop and a local art gallery.

8. **Truth or Consequences** (191 miles): **Why?** Originally called Hot Springs, it changed its name in 1950 after taking the bet to change its name from the popular TV show of the same name. T or C is known for its hot springs with ten commercial bathhouses with hot springs in the very walkable historic hot springs district. It now has a population of around 6,000.

9. **White Sands National Park** (200 miles): **Why?** When first seen at a

distance, the absolutely white what-the-heck-is-that is startling and unexpected. The park is huge covering 145,762 acres in the Tularosa Basin, including the southern 41% of a 275 sq mi field of white sand dunes composed of gypsum crystals. In addition to having the world's largest gypsum dune field and gypsum hearth mounds found nowhere else on earth, the park is home to the world's largest collection of Ice-Age fossilized footprints which are more than 20,000 years old. Because The White Sands Missile Range surrounds White Sands National Park, the park will occasionally close temporarily while missiles fly overhead. Probably a good thing.

10. **The Lightning Field** (203 miles): **Why?** In 1977, the American sculptor Walter De Maria installed 400 polished two-inch diameter, stainless-steel poles with pointed tips, ranging from 15 feet to 26 feet 9 inches in height, set exactly 220 feet apart from one another in a grid measuring one mile by one kilometer (I know, strange). It is set in a remote area about 40 miles from the nearest town. The view is so exceptional because all the poles look like they are at the same height, even though this area has varying elevations. This phenomenon is called an 'isocephaly effect' and is made possible because the poles were set at different heights to compensate for the height variations. Each steel rod is set in concrete three feet deep and one foot in diameter and designed to survive winds of up to 110 miles an hour. Despite its name, this art installation does not require lightning to be appreciated.

Visitors are encouraged to spend time in the field, especially during sunset and sunrise. The Dia Art Foundation commissioned and maintained the field and offers overnight visits from May through October but only by reservations on a first-come, first-served basis, starting with requests submitted on February 1, and limited to one night per visiting group. Don't think about camping and don't bring your camera as both are prohibited.

11. **Spaceport America** (288 miles): **Why?** This is an active test facility that is closed to public access. Launches at the site are not open to public viewing and are subject to scheduling changes, but anyone wanting to view spaceflights in person can do so by using Spaceport America's public viewing lot. Private tours of the facilities can be arranged in advance through Final Frontier Tours. With Virgin Galactic's launch of the VSS *Unity* with three people aboard on May 22, 2021, New Mexico became the third US state to launch humans into space (after California and

Florida). In June 2023, Spaceport America's anchor tenant, Virgin Galactic, began monthly spaceflights from the world's first purpose-built commercial spaceport.

Driving Trails of Santa Fe

The Santa Fe National Historic Trail started in Independence, Missouri, and ended in Santa Fe. It was in continuous use between 1821 and 1880 as an important route for stagecoach travel, stagecoach mail delivery, and as a mail route for the Pony Express. From 1821 until 1846, the Santa Fe Trail was an international commercial highway used by both Mexican and American traders. The use of the trail stopped in 1880 when The Atchison, Topeka, and Santa Fe Railroad reached Santa Fe, marking the end of the Santa Fe Trail.

Turquoise Trail National Scenic Byway This beautiful drive is approximately 50 miles along Highway 14 with great views from the top of Sandia Crest. Once there, drive back and stop at the mining towns of Golden, Madrid, and Cerrillos, which are now filled with art, crafts, theater, music, museums, and restaurants.

Distance by Car From Santa Fe:

- Amarillo, Texas 279 miles
- Colorado Springs, Colorado 322 miles
- El Paso, Texas 329 miles
- Ciudad Juarez, Mexico 339 miles
- Flagstaff, Arizona 383 miles
- Phoenix, Arizona 480 miles
- San Diego, California 832 miles
- Los Angeles, California 848 miles
- San Francisco, California 1,145 miles
- Portland, Oregon 1,366 miles
- Atlanta, Georgi 1,382 miles

- Mexico City, Mexico 1,420 miles
- Seattle, Washington 1,452 miles
- Vancouver, Canada 1,588 miles
- New York City, NY 1,983 miles
- Key West, Florida 2,106 miles
- Boston, Massachusetts 2,223 miles
- Bangor, Maine 2,449 miles
- Panama Canal, Panama 3,422 miles
- Buenos Aires, Argentina 5,739 miles
- Ushuaia, Argentina 6,634 miles

**Vacoas-Phoenix, Mauritius, 11,030 miles, is the furthest town in the world from Santa Fe, but it's a really tough drive.

No Money? No Problem!
So Much to Do and See. So Little Time.

- Browse the Native American art stalls under the Portal of the Palace of the Governors. The market is located under the portal every day from 8:30 am to 5 pm.
- Attend book readings at Collected Works Bookstore, Garcia Street Books, and Travel Bug
- See the Cathedral Basilica of St. Francis of Assisi
- Bataan Memorial Military Museum, New Mexico Military Museum
- The Bataan Memorial Military Museum is located at 1050 Old Pecos Trail. Free
- Walk around Fort Marcy Park
- Walk your dog at the Frank Ortiz Dog Park, the largest off-leash dog park in the United States at 138 acres (www.thedogparkproject.org)
- Attend Canyon Road gallery openings on Friday evening

- Hike the many trails
- Visit the Santa Fe Library
- Visit the New Mexico Military Museum
- Visit the New Mexico State Capitol (The Roundhouse). This has an amazing NM art collection
- See the petroglyphs near the airport
- Walk around the Railyard Arts District
- Visit the Randall Davey Audubon Center and Sanctuary
- See the San Miguel Chapel
- Browse the Santa Fe Farmer's Market
- Attend Santa Fe Institute lectures
- Visit Santa Fe National Cemetery
- Walk around Santa Fe Plaza
- Visit Santa Fe Spirits Distillery
- Visit SITE SANTA FE
- Attend St. John's College lectures
- Stroll through Jackalope Mercado
- See the New Mexico Capitol Art Collection of contemporary art
- Visit museums on Museum Hill on specific free days for seniors and NM residents
- Walk Canyon Road to see 100 galleries
- Walk around the Railyard to explore art galleries, unique shops, restaurants, and a movie theater.

Consignment Stores!
Explore some of the best in the US!

- 801 Boutique

- Act 2
- Art.i.fact
- Bohemiac Santa Fe
- Congeries Consignment
- Consignment Warehouse
- Double Take
- Encore 505
- Just U Antiques
- Kitchenality
- La Casa Fina Consignment and Antiques
- La Familia 821
- On Canyon Road Consignment Gallery
- Ooh La La Consignment
- Real Deal Collection
- Santa Fe Fine Consign
- Santa Fe Vintage
- Santa Fe Vintage Outpost
- Stephens: A Consignment Gallery
- The Cat and The Cat South
- The Raven Fine Consignments
- Valdez Santa Fe Antiques Consignments

Chapter 4

PEOPLE, PEOPLE, PEOPLE

THE BACKSTORY
of Places, Names, and Buildings

Agua Fria (cold water) was the old Camino Real, one of the oldest trade routes in the US, going from Veracruz to Mexico City to Chihuahua to Santa Fe.

Buckman Road was named for Henry Buckman who had a successful timber-cutting business in the early 1900s.

The Compound Restaurant was an adobe home that was the main home in a group of houses known as the McComb Compound before it changed into a restaurant in 1966.

DeVargas Mall: The mall was named for the Spanish Governor of New Mexico, Don Diego de Vargas (1643-1704).

Don Gaspar Avenue was named after Don Gaspar Ortiz y Alarid (1835-1882), a merchant who ran wagon trains from Santa Fe to Chihuahua and St. Louis, Missouri. He granted the right of way through one of his fields for this street.

Doodlet's was Will Shuster's nickname for Theo Raven when she was a baby. She opened Doodlet's in 1955.

Evangelo's was named for Evangelo Klonis, who opened Evangelo's in 1970. He appeared on the cover of Life Magazine in an iconic WWII photograph while he served in the army.

Geronimo Restaurant was built in 1756 by Geronimo Lopez, a soldier in the Spanish army.

Grant, Lincoln, and Washington Avenues were named for the presidents.

Guadalupe Street was named for Our Lady of Guadalupe.

Kaune's Neighborhood Market: (pronounced like the name, Connie) is an independent specialty grocery store founded by Henry S. Kaune in 1896.

La Fonda means 'The Hotel' in Spanish.

Lamy is a little Southeast of Santa Fe and got its name from Archbishop Jean Baptiste Lamy, the first archbishop of Santa Fe. He was the first owner to live on the property that would later become known as The Bishop's Lodge. He built the Santa Fe Saint Francis Cathedral and had a major influence on Catholicism in the region until he died in 1888. Willa Cather's novel *Death Comes for the Archbishop,* was based on Bishop Lamy's life.

Marcy Street was named for William Marcy, Secretary of War under President James Polk

Pacheco Street is named after Jose de la Cruz Pacheco

Palace Avenue is named for the Palace of the Governors.

Paseo de Peralta is named for Don Pedro Peralta, who founded and gave the city its name. He also planned the city, including the plaza for government buildings.

Pasqual's Restaurant (later Café Pasqual's) is named after San Pasqual, the folk saint of Mexican kitchens and chefs.

The Roundhouse is the nickname for New Mexico's state capital building because, well, it's round. In fact, it is the only round capital building in the United States. It opened in 1966 and houses both chambers of the New Mexico Legislature and the offices of the Governor, Lieutenant Governor, and the Secretary of State. From the top looking down, the Roundhouse resembles the Zia, the sun symbol.

San Ysidro is the patron saint of farmers.

Vladem Museum is named for philanthropists Robert and Ellen Vladem, who moved to Santa Fe from Chicago in 2013. Robert Vladem is a self-made businessman, and Ellen Vladem is a retired emergency room and oncology nurse. They have given extensively to the Santa Fe arts, including their namesake New Mexico Museum of Art Vladem Contemporary.

Zepol Road is Lopez spelled backward.

GIANTS OF SANTA FE

✒ **Fray Angélico** (1910–1996) was an author and historian. His real name was Manuel Ezequiel Chávez, but used Angelico as a pen name. He was a Hispanic American Friar, priest, historian, author, poet, and painter, but was best known for being a historian, spending his life researching New Mexico history. During WWII and the Korean War, he was a chaplain in the army. After the war, he was appointed archivist of the Archdiocese of Santa Fe. He wrote non-fiction, *But Time and Chance,* about the families of New Mexico and *La Conquistadora: The Autobiography of an Ancient Statue.* He also wrote fiction, *When the Santos Talked, From an Altar Screen,* and *Lady from Toledo;* and poetry, "The Virgin of Port Lligat" and "Cantares: Canticles and Poems of Youth." A bronze statue of Chávez by artist Donna Quasthoff stands on Washington Avenue outside the building that currently houses the library and photo archives of the New Mexico History Museum.

✒ **Witter Bynner** (1881-1968) was a poet and a social center in Santa Fe who had a major impact on the literary scene in Santa Fe. In 1911, he was the Harvard Phi Beta Kappa Poet. He introduced Kahlil Gibran to his publisher, Alfred A. Knopf, leading to the publication of *The Prophet* in 1923. He published The *Beloved Stranger, Pins for Wings, Indian Earth,* and translated the *Tao Te Ching: The Way of Life According to Lao Tsu* (1949). He briefly taught at the University of California, Berkeley (1918–1919). In 1922, he moved to Santa Fe, where he and his partner Robert Hunt hosted gatherings for artists and literary figures like D.H. Lawrence, Georgia O'Keeffe, Robert Frost, and Carl Sandburg at their home, which is now The Inn of the Turquoise Bear.

✒ **Cinco Pintores** (The Five Painters) was a group of artists who founded the Santa Fe art society called Los Cinco Pintores in the 1920s. The five included Will Shuster (**1893-1969**), Fremont Ellis (1897-1985), Walter Mruk (1883-1942), Jozef Bakos (1891-1977), and Willard Nash (1898-1943). They became influential in the art movement in Santa Fe with their first exhibition held at the New Mexico Museum of Art in 1921 but the group disbanded in 1926. Artist William Howard "Will" Shuster, Jr. created the first Zozobra in 1924 as the highlight for a private party of the Cinco Pintores. Shuster was inspired by the Easter Holy Week tradition in the Yaqui Indian communities of Arizona and Mexico, in which an effigy of Judas is led around the village on a donkey and ultimately set alight. Shuster and his friend, E. Dana Johnson, editor of The Santa Fe New Mexican, came up with the name "Zozobra." They were called the "five nuts in mud huts" because they all built their homes.

- **Mary Colter** (1869-1958) was one of the very few female architects of her time. She designed landmark buildings and spaces for the Fred Harvey Company and the Santa Fe Railroad. Her work blended elements of Spanish Colonial Revival, Mission Revival, and Native American styles. She contributed to redesigning the La Fonda Hotel, giving it her unique style and designing many historic buildings in the Grand Canyon and the La Posada Hotel in Winslow, Arizona. She championed Native American cultures, which had a major influence on her designs. She retired to Santa Fe.

- **John O. Crosby** (1926-2002) founded The Santa Fe Opera in 1956 and remained active as director until 2000, making him the longest-running general director of an opera company in the United States at 44 years. Crosby's path to Santa Fe was influenced by a bout of asthma during his early studies in Connecticut. He attended the Los Alamos Ranch School in New Mexico, sparking his love for the Santa Fe area. At Yale University, Crosby studied composition and musical arrangements for theatrical productions. In 1956, he founded the Santa Fe Opera Association and planned for an outside opera. Crosby bought the San Juan Ranch, a 199-acre guest ranch near Santa Fe where he built the first opera house that was designed exclusively for outdoor performances.

- **Dr. Edgar L. Hewett** (1865–1946) was an artist, anthropologist, and archaeologist who founded and was the first director of the Museum of New Mexico. He was appointed as the first president of the New Mexico Normal School, later becoming New Mexico Highlands University. He delivered an influential report on conservation to Congress in 1904 and submitted a "Memorandum concerning the historic and prehistoric ruins of Arizona, New Mexico, Colorado, and Utah, and their preservation" to the United States General Land Office (GLO), which had jurisdiction over government lands in the Southwest. Both influenced Congress to pass the Antiquities Act of 1906, which helped protect cultural resources.

⤴ **Allan Houser** (1914-1994) was one of America's most influential modernist sculptors of the 20th century. His pieces can be found at the Smithsonian Museum of American Art, the National Museum of the American Indian, the National Portrait Gallery in Washington, D.C., the Oklahoma State Capitol Building, and many major museum collections throughout North America, Europe, and Japan. His sculpture, *Offering of the Sacred Pipe,* is on display at the United States Mission to the United Nations in New York City. In 2018, he became one of the first inductees in the National Native American Hall of Fame and was the first Native American awarded the National Medal of Arts. He was Sculpture Department Head and taught at the Institute of American Indian Arts from 1962 to 1975. He lived in Santa Fe from 1962 on.

⤴ **Oliver La Farge** (1901–1963) was a writer and anthropologist. He graduated from Harvard with a bachelor's and master's degree. He won the Pulitzer Prize for fiction for *Laughing Boy* in 1929 and wrote many other fiction and non-fiction books. He became an advocate for American Indian rights and was president of the Association on American Indian Affairs for years. He is one of the reasons that Santa Fe has such a robust public library system, with the Llano branch named after him. He was a long-time resident of Santa Fe. His son, Pen La Farge, is an author in his own right, publishing *Turn Left at the Sleeping Dog* in 2006, and, like his father, Pen is a huge advocate for historic preservation. He lives in Santa Fe.

⤴ **Murray Gell-Mann** (1928-2019) was an American physicist who won the Nobel Prize for Physics in 1969 for his work on the classification of subatomic particles and their interactions. At age 15, he entered Yale University, graduated with a B.S. in physics in 1948, and then earned a Ph.D. in 1951 at the Massachusetts Institute of Technology. He was also a member of the board of directors of Encyclopædia Britannica. In 1984 he cofounded the Santa Fe Institute.

⤴ **Maria Concepcion Ortiz y Pino de Kleven** (1910-2006) served in the New Mexico Legislature, where she was the youngest American woman elected to state office and the third Hispanic woman legislator in the United States. President John F. Kennedy appointed her to the National Council of Upward Bound.

⤳ **Lars** (1856-1931) **and Belle** (1858-1892) **Larson** founded the New Mexico School for the Deaf (NMSD) in 1885. Lars was a graduate of Gallaudet College. Both Lars and Belle were deaf and started teaching deaf students in Santa Fe using their own money. In 1887, their school was taken over by the State of New Mexico, making it the first public school in Santa Fe. Lars was the NMSD Superintendent until 1906.

⤳ **Jean-Baptiste Lamy** (1814–1888) was the first Archbishop of Santa Fe. He was a native of France but was living in Cincinnati when he was appointed bishop. He is a somewhat controversial figure, with some Catholics finding him a hero while others find him the villain. Lamy built the Cathedral Basilica of Saint Francis of Assisi in Santa Fe, where he is buried beneath the floor. He is also responsible for bringing apricot trees and lilac bushes to Santa Fe, which he had brought with him from France.

⤳ **Albina Lucero** (1879-1957) was appointed the first female Deputy Sheriff in 1926. Her job was to guard female prisoners at the local jail and supervise local dances and community events. In addition to being a *midwife,* Lucero was also a *curandera* (holistic healer). In the 1930s, Lucero received a certificate from the Department of Health for assisting hundreds of women during childbirth.

⤳ **Maria Martinez** (1887-1980) was born and died in the San Ildefonso Pueblo, in Santa Fe. Maria Martinez is one of the best-known and most influential Native American potters of the 1900s who developed the "black-on-black" style of pottery. She **was awarded two honorary doctorates, had her portrait made by the American sculptor Malvina Hoffman, and in 1978, had a major exhibition by the Smithsonian Institution's Renwick Gallery.**

⤳ **John Gaw Meem** (1894–1983) is considered by many to be New Mexico's greatest 20th-century architect, but he didn't even start as an architect. He was born and raised in Brazil and graduated with a Civil Engineering degree from the Virginia Military Institute because of family tradition. He then moved to Brooklyn, New York, to work on the subway system. During WWI, he was called up as an officer. After leaving the army, he joined the National City Bank of New York and was sent to Brazil, where he contracted tuberculosis. He went to Santa Fe's Sunmount Sanatorium to recover, where he began to appreciate Pueblo and Territorial architecture which made him move to Denver to get experience as an architect. When he had a TB relapse, he moved back to Santa Fe, where he popularized the Pueblo Revival style. He designed the La Fonda Hotel, 35 major buildings at the University of New Mexico, the Fuller Lodge in Los Alamos, Cristo Rey Church in Santa Fe, and the buildings at Los Poblanos. He designed the campus and many buildings of the Santa Fe campus of St. John's College which opened on land donated primarily by John Gaw Meem. He was a long-time resident of Santa Fe.

☙ **Pamela B. Minzer** (1943-2007) was a graduate of Harvard Law School and a tenured full professor at UNM Law School; author; New Mexico Court of Appeals judge, the court's Chief Judge, a justice on the New Mexico Supreme Court, and its first female Chief Justice.

☙ **N. Scott Momaday** (1934-2024) was a poet, essayist, and storyteller. He was a Pulitzer Prize-winning author for *"House Made of Dawn"* in 1969. He graduated from the University of New Mexico and received a Ph.D. at Stanford University. As Loren Kieve, Chair of the board of trustees of the Institute of American Indian Arts, stated, "Momaday inspired generations of Indigenous readers, writers, educators, and the public by bringing the Indigenous experience to literature, which continues to motivate IAIA students, staff, faculty, and alums." He had a long academic career, getting tenure at the University of California, Santa Barbara, The University of Arizona, and the University of California-Berkley. He was the first professor to teach American Literature in Moscow, Russia at Moscow State University.

☙ **Georgia O'Keeffe** (1887-1986) was among the most influential artists in Modernism, best known for her large-format paintings of natural subjects, especially flowers and bones, and for her depictions of architecture and landscapes unique to northern New Mexico. O'Keeffe also played a key role in changing the art community's and the general public's attitude that gender had nothing to do with artistic competence or creativity, helping female artists find their voice in a male-dominated industry.

In 1977, President Gerald Ford presented O'Keeffe with the Presidential Medal of Freedom, the highest honor awarded to American civilians. In 1985, she was awarded the National Medal of Arts by President Ronald

Reagan, and in 1993, she was inducted into the National Women's Hall of Fame. The Georgia O'Keeffe Museum opened in Santa Fe in 1997. A fossilized species of archosaur was named *Effigia okeeffeae* ("O'Keeffe's Ghost") in January 2006, "in honor of Georgia O'Keeffe for her numerous paintings of the badlands at Ghost Ranch and her interest in the Coelophysis Quarry when it was discovered."

◟ **Gerald Peters** might be a somewhat controversial figure, but he has undoubtedly had a tremendous influence in Santa Fe through real estate, art galleries, and his remaking of today's downtown.

◟ **Jean Seth** (1922-2013) opened the first gallery on Canyon Road in the early 1960s. Her Friday night gallery openings at Jean Seth Gallery could draw as many as 1,000 people.

◟ **William Shuster, Jr.** (1893-1969) was a painter, sculptor, and teacher. He served in the U.S. Army during World War I in France, where he contracted tuberculosis after being exposed to mustard gas. In 1920, he moved to New Mexico to improve his health. In 1921, Shuster became a member of Los Cinco Pintores ("the five painters"), a group of artists in Santa Fe who exhibited their work throughout Santa Fe and the rest of the country. He created the first Zozobra in his backyard on Camino del Monte Sol. His artwork is part of the permanent collections of several museums, including the Stark Museum of Art, Brooklyn Museum, Delaware Art Museum, Newark Museum, and New Mexico Museum of Art.

◟ **Carlos Vierra** (1876-1937) was Santa Fe's first non-indigenous resident artist and one of the first three Santa Fe Art Colony members. He was a Portuguese-American painter and photographer. In 1909, the School of American Archaeology's director, Edgar Lee Hewett, appointed Vierra to manage the building of the New Mexico Museum of Art (formerly the Museum of Fine Arts). He had an influential role in restoring the Palace of the Governors, the oldest capitol building in the United States. Additionally, he painted three murals in the St. Francis Auditorium. In 1914, he was commissioned to paint each of the Pueblo mission churches, which showed both Spanish and Pueblo traditional New Mexico architecture. His house in Santa Fe is considered the first purposefully designed Spanish Pueblo Revival-style residence.

◟ **Donaciano Vigil** (1802-1877) was a former Territorial Governor of New

Mexico 1847-1851). He called for the establishment of a public school system open to the poor as well as the rich and called for the creation of a public university. He helped with the peaceful transition from Mexico to the United States. He served 25 years in the US Army starting as a private and rising to the rank of captain.

- **Don Diego de Vargas** (1643-1704) was a governor of New Mexico. The Pueblo Revolt in 1680 resulted in the Spanish losing control of New Mexico, which kept the Spanish out of New Mexico for 12 years. In 1692, DeVargas and his Spanish soldiers took the territory back in what is known as the "bloodless battle," meaning no Spanish soldiers were killed. But, later, in 1693, DeVargas had to return to the area again to put down mounting resistance to Spanish settlers. The Spanish were successful, but this battle was the opposite of bloodless, with two days of fierce fighting. After the fighting, De Vargas executed everyone who did not surrender, and those who did surrender were required to be slaves for 10 years. On June 18, 2020, the city of Santa Fe removed the Statue of Diego de Vargas that had been erected 150 years earlier.

- **Mary Cabot Wheelwright** *(1878-1958) was an American anthropologist and museum founder.* In 1937, Wheelwright and Hosteen Klah established the House of Navajo Religion in Santa Fe but changed the name to the Museum of Navajo Ceremonial Art in 1939. In 1942, the museum published *Navajo Creation Myth - the Story of the Emergence* by Hosteen Klah and recorded by Mary C. Wheelwright. In 1977, the museum was renamed the Wheelwright Museum of the American Indian. The museum is no longer actively involved in the study of Navajo religion but maintains world-class collections that document Navajo art and culture from 1850 to the present.

- **The White Sisters** Amelia Elizabeth White (1878–1972) and Martha White (died 1937). They moved to Santa Fe from New York after graduating from Bryn Mahr. They had a house on Garcia, known as El Delirio (The Madness), where they threw lavish parties for some of the most famous people in the United States. She founded Santa Fe's first animal shelter and worked with the U.S. Army to develop World War II's "Dogs for Defense" sentry program. Upon her death in 1972, she gave El Delirio to the School for Advanced Research (SAR), which is still in its present location. For more, read *The Artistry of El Delirio: The White*

Sisters' Remarkable Legacy by Nancy Owen Lewis.

✒ **Three Wise Women** are three generations of women who built the Acequia Madre House: Eva Scott Fényes, her daughter, Leonora S. M. Curtin, and granddaughter, Leonora F. Curtin, who later married Yrjö Paloheimo of Finland. Fényes, who first came to Santa Fe in the 1880s, was a businesswoman and visual artist and her daughter Leonora Curtin became a widely recognized ethnobotanist and author. Her daughter, also named Leonora, became a linguistics scholar who documented Native American languages, as well as a founder of the Native Market in Santa Fe during the Depression. Over 150 years, these three women studied and participated in cultural conservation, including ethnobotany of Northern New Mexico, Native American languages and songs, Western and Southwestern architecture, and the arts and folk arts of the United States and Finland.

✒ **Zozobra** (Spanish for doom, gloom, and anguish) or "Old Man Gloom" is meant to be part ghost and part monster. It was created by Will Shuster, Jr., in his backyard in 1924 as a 6-foot effigy but has grown to 50 feet, making it one of the biggest marionettes in the world. It is burned to get rid of the gloom and agony of the past year so that a fresh start can be had in the new year. Zozobra's burning occurs at Fort Marcy Park on Friday of Labor Day Weekend. In 1964, Will Shuster handed over Zozobra to the Kiwanis Club of Santa Fe in perpetuity.

PEOPLE YOU KNOW & DON'T KNOW

But all have made an impact on Santa Fe

A Very Partial List

Activists

- **Nina Otero-Warren** (1881-1965) was the first woman superintendent of Santa Fe public schools and an activist for women's suffrage. One of only four women honored on the face of a US coin.

- **Charlene Teters** (born 1952) is a Native American artist, educator, and lecturer who has actively opposed Native American mascots and other imagery in sports since 1989. She has an Associate of Fine Arts in Painting from the Institute of American Indian Arts (IAIA) and a Bachelor of Fine Arts in Painting from the College of Santa Fe (later Santa Fe University of Art and Design).

- **Miguel Trujillo** *(1904-1989)* played an instrumental role in *Trujillo v Garley (1948)*, which granted Native American New Mexicans the right to vote in US elections. The ruling in 1948 removed legal and constitutional barriers to voting for Native Americans residing on tribal lands in New Mexico.

Architecture

- **Mary Elizabeth Jane Colter** (1869-1958) was the principal architect and interior designer for the Fred Harvey Company from 1902 to 1948. She was responsible for the historical design of the La Fonda Hotel. One of the most visionary architects and interior designers of her time in what was a male-dominated industry. She was one of the guiding forces behind National Park Service Rustic-style architecture, believing a building should grow organically out of its environment. She retired to Santa Fe in 1948.

⌐ **Tjalke Charles Gaastra** (1879–1947) was an architect in the Pueblo Revival Style. He won the International Exhibit of Architecture in Berlin for the Gildersleeve house in Santa Fe, which he designed for David Chavez, New Mexico Supreme Court Justice. His other well-known buildings include the Cassell Building, the Bishop's Lodge, Gormley Elementary School, and the Gustave Baumann House in Santa Fe; the Wool Warehouse, Monte Vista Elementary School, the Carlisle Gymnasium, the Hendren Building, and the old Bernalillo County Courthouse in Albuquerque; and the Theatre Building built for Jack Brandenburg in Taos. Several of his buildings are listed in the National Register of Historic Places.

⌐ **John Brinckerhoff Jackson** (1909–1996) was a landscape architect, writer, publisher, instructor, and sketch artist in landscape design. He was the publisher and editor of *Landscape* from 1951 to 1968. Jackson lived in La Cienega, near a historic property known as El Rancho de las Golondrinas (The Ranch of the Swallows). He died in 1996 at St. Vincent Hospital in Santa Fe.

Archaeology

⌐ **Adolph Bandelier** (1840-1914) was an archaeologist. The Bandelier National Monument, containing prehistoric homes of the later Pueblo period, was established in 1916. He lived in the Kaune-Bandelier House from 1882 to 1891 while conducting research in New Mexico and Mexico.

⌐ **Sylvanus Morley** (1883–1948) was an archaeologist and Mayanist. During WWI, he worked for ONI (Office of Naval Intelligence) as a spy (Agent 53) and it has been suggested that he could have been the role model for Indiana Jones. Morley's research library was preserved and available for research at the Laboratory of Anthropology Library in Santa Fe. He was an influential Santa Fe Planning Board member when it decided to adopt a unified building style, "The Santa Fe Style."

⌐ **Jesse L. Nusbaum** (1887–1975) was an archaeologist, anthropologist, photographer, and National Park Service Superintendent. He was the first archeologist hired by the National Park Service and supervised the restoration of the New Mexico Palace of Governors in Santa Fe, which was completed in 1913. In 1958, Nusbaum retired to write and work at his home on Camino del Monte Sol.

Art

~ **Gustave Baumann** (1881–1971) was a printmaker, marionette-maker, painter, and resident artist for more than fifty years. He made the head of the first Zozobra and was a member of the Society of American Graphic Artists and the Taos Society of Artists. He remained in Santa Fe for more than fifty years.

~ **William Berra** (born 1952) is a painter of landscapes, figures, and still life. His work is in galleries throughout the United States, and he is a long-time resident of Santa Fe.

~ **Ned Bittinger** (born 1951) is a portrait painter and illustrator who lived in Santa Fe. He was commissioned to paint Henry Kissinger's portrait and the official portrait of Abraham Lincoln by the US House of Representatives.

~ **Paul Burlin** (1886–1969) was a modern and abstract expressionist painter. His work was included in the New York Museum of Modern Art's Ninth Exhibition of Painting and Sculpture by Living Americans in 1930. He lived in Santa Fe from 1913 to 1920.

~ **Dana B. Chase** (1848–1897) was a photographer whose photographs are in the permanent collections of the Getty Museum, the Amon Carter Museum, the Autry Museum of the American West, and the Harwood Museum of Art. The New Mexico History Museum Palace of the Governor's photo archives holds 230 of his photographic prints, including images of Santa Fe during the territorial period, the Pueblo people, and other New Mexico scenes. His gallery was on the Plaza.

~ **Laura Gilpin** (1891–1979) was a photographer and author. Ten of Gilpin's photographs were purchased by the Library of Congress. She wrote several books, including *The Pueblos: A Camera Chronicle of Hichen Itza* (1948), *The Rio Grande: River of Destiny* (1949), and *The Enduring Navaho* (1987). She was chairman of the Indian Arts Fund in Santa Fe (1958) Santa Fe. She lived in Santa Fe.

~ **Glenna Goodacre** (1939-2020) was a sculptor who designed the Vietnam Women's Memorial in Washington, D.C., and the front face (obverse) of the US Sacagawea dollar that entered circulation in 2000. She lived in Santa Fe.

- **William Penhallow Henderson** (1877-1943) was a painter and architect who was commissioned by Frank Lloyd Wright to design Murals for Midway Gardens in Chicago. He was also one of the founders of the New Mexico Painters Society and, remarkably, painted camouflage onto ship hulls during WWI. During the 1920s, he formed a building company to design and construct buildings and fine furniture in the Santa Fe area. He and his wife, Alice Corbin, lived in Santa from 1916 on.

- **Matt King** (1984-2022) was an artist, Senior Creative Director, and co-founder of Meow Wolf. He was involved with over 34 Meow Wolf projects, many as the lead artist, including Fancy Town, Wiggy's Plasma Plex video arcade, and Glowquarium. He was a long-time resident of Santa Fe.

- **Hosteen Klah** (1867-1937) was a Native American and medicine man, primarily known for his sand painting weavings. Because of a friendship with Mary Cabot Wheelwright, they formed the Museum of Navajo Ceremonial Art in 1937, known today as the Wheelwright Museum. Most of his sand painting weavings were returned to Navajo Nation. He is buried on the grounds of the Wheelwright Museum.

- **Christine McHorse** (1948–2021) was a Navajo ceramic artist. From 1963 to 1968, she studied at the Institute of American Indian Arts (IAIA) in Santa Fe, where it was a high school for the arts on the campus of the Santa Fe Indian School. She exhibited at Santa Fe Indian Market for 23 years, winning 38 awards for both pottery and sculpture. Her work can be found in the permanent collections of the Heard Museum, the Denver Art Museum, the National Museum of the American Indian, the Navajo Nation Museum, and others. Her work is also featured in the catalog *Dark Light: The Ceramics of Christine Nofchissey McHorse*. She lived and died in Santa Fe.

- **John Nieto** (1936–2018) was an American contemporary artist who used lots of color to depict Native American themes. In 1994, he received the New Mexico Governor's Award for Achievement in the Arts. He served on the advisory boards for both the Wheelwright Museum and the Native American Preparatory School. His work is shown in the New Mexico Museum of Fine Arts. He was a longtime resident of Santa Fe.

~ **Hib Sabin** (born 1935) is known for his indigenous-style sculptures in juniper wood. His work includes spirit animal spirit bowls, spirit canoes, dream and dance sticks, and shamanistic masks. He lives in Santa Fe.

~ **Fritz Scholder** (1937-2005) was a native American artist and a teacher at the Institute of American Indian Arts (IAIA) from 1964 to 1969. He was a major influence on native American artists. In 2009, Governor Arnold Schwarzenegger and First Lady Maria Shriver announced that Scholder was one of 13 California Hall of Fame inductees. He had a home and studio on Canyon Road.

~ **Jean Seth** (1922-2013) opened the first art gallery on Canyon Road in the early 1960s. She served on the first Santa Fe Opera board, the Georgia O'Keeffe Museum and the Northern Arizona University Museum, the Women's Board of the Museum of New Mexico, and the Smithsonian National Museum of Art advisory board.

~ **Charlene Teters** (born 1952) is a Native American artist and activist. She graduated from the Institute of American Indian Arts and the College of Santa Fe (later the Santa Fe University of Art and Design). She was honored as "Person of the Week" by Peter Jennings on the *ABC World News Tonight* program for her commitment to her work and her people. She was the first artist-in-residence at the American Museum of Natural History in New York City, New York. She lives in Santa Fe.

Authors

~ **Mary Hunter Austin** (1868–1934) was an author. She helped establish The Santa Fe Little Theatre (The Santa Fe Playhouse). In 1929, while living in New Mexico, Austin co-authored a book with photographer Ansel Adams, *Taos Pueblo*. Her home at 439 Camino del Monte Sol is listed on the National Register of Historic Places as a contributing building in the Camino del Monte Sol Historic District.

~ **Witter Bynner** (1881–1968) was a poet who served as president of the Poetry Society of America from 1921 to 1923. Together with his life-long partner, Robert Hun (1906-1964), they entertained artists and literary figures such as Ansel Adams, W. H. Auden, Willa Cather, Robert Frost, Martha Graham, Aldous Huxley, Christopher Isherwood, D. H. Lawrence and his wife, Edna St. Vincent Millay, James Merrill, Georgia

O'Keeffe, Carl Sandburg, Igor Stravinsky, Carl Van Vechten, and Thornton Wilder. He lived in Santa Fe from 1922 on.

ℐ **Julia Cameron** (1948) is the author of *The Artist's Way, The Vein of Gold,* and *The Right to Write.* She is James Cameron's sister and lives in Santa Fe.

ℐ **Willa Cather** (1873-1947) was an author probably best known for *Death Comes for the Archbishop, O Pioneers!* and *My Antonia,* but she won the Pulitzer Prize for *One of Ours.* She was the first woman to receive an honorary degree from Princeton, and she appeared on the cover of *Time Magazine* in 1931. She spent a considerable amount of time in Santa Fe in the 1920s and 1930s.

ℐ **Evan S. Connell** (1924-2013) was a National Book Award finalist, a member of the American Academy of Arts and Letters, and a finalist in 2009 for the International Man Booker Award for lifetime achievement. His best-known books included his first novel, *Mrs. Bridge.* Paul Newman and Joanne Woodward appeared in the 1990 film *Mr. & Mrs. Bridge,* based on Connell's twin novels, each written from the title character's perspective. He lived in Santa Fe from 1989 until his death in 2013.

ℐ **Forrest Fenn** (1930-2020) was an author and artifacts dealer. He was a major in the US Air Force with 328 combat missions flown during the Vietnam War. After the war, he opened an art gallery in Santa Fe. When he was diagnosed with cancer, he decided to hide a treasure chest somewhere north of Santa Fe. In 2010, he published *The Thrill of the Chase: A Memoir,* which he said held clues to the location of the treasure chest. The treasure chest was discovered on June 16, 2020, in Wyoming. In December 2022, an auction of the contents netted $1.3 million. Five people died trying to find the treasure.

ℐ **Dorothy B. Hughes** (1904–1993) was a crime writer, literary critic, and historian. Several of Hughes's novels were adapted as Hollywood films: *The Fallen Sparrow* (1943), *Ride the Pink Horse* (1947), and *In A Lonely Place* (1950). She lived in Santa Fe in the 1960s.

ℐ **Jeffe Kennedy** (born 1966) is a fantasy romance author who has written more than 15 titles, including the *Twelve Kingdoms* and the *Uncharted Realms* series. He lives in Santa Fe

ℐ **Marjorie Herrera Lewis** (born 1957) is the author of the 2018 novel

When the Men Were Gone, which Sports Illustrated called the best sports book of the year. She was the only female college football coach when she coached the defensive backs at Texas Wesleyan University and the first female beat writer to cover the Dallas Cowboys when she was with the *Fort Worth Star-Telegram*.

🖋 **George R. R. Martin** (born 1948) is the author and screenwriter of *Game of Thrones*. In 2011, he was included in the annual Time Magazine's *Time 100* list of the most influential people in the world. He helped fund Meow Wolf and owns the Jean Cocteau Cinema. He lives in Santa Fe and is often seen out and about.

🖋 **Cormac McCarthy** (1933-2023) was the author of many novels, including *All the Pretty Horses* (1992), for which he received both the National Book Award and the National Book Critics Circle Award. It was followed by *The Crossing* (1994) and *Cities of the Plain* (1998), completing *The Border Trilogy*. His 2005 novel *No Country for Old Men* was turned into a movie, and his 2006 novel *The Road* won the Pulitzer Prize for Fiction. He moved to Santa Fe to be close to the Santa Fe Institute.

🖋 **Carmella Padilla** (born 1964) is a co-founder of the Santa Fe International Literary Festival. She has written several books, including *The Work of Art: Folk Artists in the 21st Century; El Rancho de las Golondrinas: Living History in New Mexico's La Cienega Valley; Low'n Slow: Lowriding in New Mexico;* and *The Chile Chronicles: Tales of a New Mexico Harvest*.

🖋 **Douglas Preston** (1956) is an author who has written many novels, including *The Codex, Blasphemy,* and *Tyrannosaur Canyon,* as well as non-fiction books, including *The Monster of Florence: A True Story* (with Mario Spezi), *The Lost City of the Monkey God,* and the *Royal Road: El Camino Real from Mexico City to Santa Fe*. He is known for his collaboration with Lincoln Child to write the *Agent Pendergast* Series, *Gideon Crew* series, *Riptide, Thunderhead, The Ice Limit,* and others. His work has been adapted into films and television series. In 2010, he was one of the authors who participated in a USO tour sponsored by the International Thriller Writers that visited Kuwait and Iraq, making it the first time in USO's history that authors visited a combat zone. He and his family are longtime residents of Santa Fe.

🖋 **Eliot Porter** (1901–1990) was a photographer whose 1962 book, *In Wildness Is the Preservation of the World* pioneered the genre of nature photography coffee-table books. He served as a director of the Sierra Club from 1965 to 1971. He was elected a Fellow of the American Academy of Arts and Sciences in 1971. In 1979, his work was exhibited in *Intimate Landscapes*, the first one-person show of color photography at The Metropolitan Museum of Art, New York. He lived in Tesuque.

Garance Franke-Ruta (born 1972) is a journalist who worked as Washington editor of *Yahoo News* and editor in chief of *Yahoo Politics*, *Voices* columnist and politics editor of *The Atlantic* Online, national web politics editor for the *Washington Post*, senior editor at the *American Prospect*, and senior writer at the *Washington City Paper*, D.C.'s alternative weekly newspaper. Her work has also appeared in *Medium* magazine, *New York*, *The Wall Street Journal*, *The Atlantic*, *The New Republic*, *Slate*, *Salon*, *The Washington Monthly*, *Legal Affairs*, *Utne Reader*, and *National Journal*. She attended Santa Fe High School and a private high school in Santa Fe, each for one year, before obtaining a G.E.D. from the state of New Mexico in 1988. After first attending Hunter College, she transferred to Harvard University, where she graduated magna cum laude in 1997.

Hampton Sides (born 1962) is an author of narrative history and literary non-fiction, including *Blood and Thunder* (2006), *In the Kingdom of Ice* (2014), and *The Wide, Wide Sea* (2024). He divides his time between Santa Fe and Colorado College, lecturing, teaching narrative non-fiction, and serving as Journalist in Residence. He is also the 2015 Miller Distinguished Scholar at the Santa Fe Institute

Sheri S. Tepper (1929–2016) was a feminist science fiction writer, including *The Gate to Women's Country, Beauty, Grass,* and many others. In November 2015, she received the World Fantasy Award for Life Achievement. She ran a guest ranch in Santa Fe.

Michael Charles Tobias (born 1951) is an author, environmentalist, mountaineer, and filmmaker. He wrote a book, *World War III: Population and the Biosphere at the End of the Millennium* and is the President and CEO of the Dancing Star Foundation. Based on his book, he directed a feature-film documentary called *No Vacancy*, which focused on the growing world population. His more than 35 books and 100 films have been distributed, translated, and/or broadcast internationally. He once lived in Santa Fe.

ℒ **Roger Zelazny** (1937–1995) was a science fiction and fantasy writer, including *The Chronicles of Amber.* He won the Nebula Award three times and the Hugo Award 6 times. He lived in Santa Fe from the 1970s until his death.

Aviation

ℒ **Katherine Stinson** (1891-1977) was the fourth woman in the United States to earn a pilot's license and set records for aerobatic maneuvers, distance, and endurance. She was the first female pilot employed by the U.S. Postal Service, the first civilian pilot to fly mail in Canada, one of the first pilots to fly at night, and the first female pilot to fly in Asia. But wait, there's more. During WWI, she raised 2 million dollars for the Red Cross by stunt flying and then went to Europe to drive ambulances in England and France. In the early 1920s, Katherine contracted tuberculosis and checked into Santa Fe's Sunmount Sanatorium for treatment. In 1927, she married Miguel Antonio Otero Jr., a district judge and son of the former territorial governor of New Mexico. She came to love Southwest architecture, and even with no professional architectural training, she designed Dorothy McKibbin's (The Gatekeeper of Los Alamos) adobe home in Santa Fe in 1936. She lived in Santa Fe for 50 years. Later, her brothers formed the Stinson Aircraft Company, which was bought by Piper Aircraft.

ℒ **Winnie Beasley** joined the Women's Air Transport Auxiliary and ferried planes from the United States to Scotland and fighter and bomber bases in England. She also flew British-built planes from factories to bases around the nation, including B-25 bombers. During the war, she married Colonel Peter Beasley.

ℒ **Charles Lindbergh** stayed in Santa Fe while he did aerial photography of Chaco Canyon and other sites and digs for archeologists in 1929.

Bad Boys

ℒ **Billy the Kid** (1859-1881), AKA William Bonney, was the original bad boy; he was an outlaw and gunfighter and the guest of the Santa Fe County Jail from Dec. 27, 1880, to March 28, 1881.

Business

- **Antonio Armijo** (1804–1850) was an explorer and merchant who led the first commercial caravan between Santa Fe and Los Angeles in 1829–1830.

- **Sam and Ethel Ballen.** La Fonda was operating as a Harvey House until 1968 when Sam and Ethel Ballen purchased the building for one million dollars. The Ballens' invested heavily into saving the La Fonda, which had fallen into disrepair which helped save the building's historical architecture and timeless elegance.

- **Maria Gertrudis Barcelo (Doña Tules)** (1800-1852) was a wealthy Santa Fe gambling hall owner and gambler in the 1830s and 1840s. After the invasion of New Mexico in 1846, the US Army had to borrow money from her to pay its troops, making the occupation of Santa Fe possible. A 1962 episode of Death Valley Days, "La Tules," was about her. Her establishment was known for its opulence and attracted visitors from various walks of life and had as its motto, "Sustenance for man and beasts." Her gambling hall was in what is now the Palace Prime Restaurant.

- **Don Felipe Chavez** (El Milloinario) (1834-1906) was a successful businessman and entrepreneur who became one of the wealthiest people in New Mexico. He lived in Santa Fe.

- **Jean Baptiste LeLande** (1778–1821) left Indiana in 1804 with merchandise for Santa Fe, and as a result, is credited as being the first American to establish commercial contact with Santa Fe. At that time Santa Fe was Spanish territory and Spanish law prohibited foreign trading. Sure enough, when he arrived in New Mexico, he was arrested by Spanish authorities, and his goods were seized. The Spanish governor released LaLande from prison in 1805. He died in Santa Fe in 1821.

- **Earl and Deborah Potter.** In May 1998, they opened the first Five & Dime General Store in the location of the original Woolworth's in Santa Fe. Today, the Five and Dime is a chain of nine. The Potters have a sense of humor since their Five & Dime General Stores are owned and operated by UTBW ("Used To Be Woolworth's") LLC. Deborah's mother, British-American actress Joan Fontaine, starred in several films in the late 1930's and early 40's and is best known for her role in Alfred Hitchcock's *Rebecca* and won an Academy Award for her role in *Suspicion* with

Cary Grant. Her mother's elder sister, actress Olivia deHavilland, played "Melanie" in *Gone With the Wind*.

↵ **Garrett Thornburg** (born 1946) graduated from Harvard and founded Thornburg Investment Management, a global investment firm based in Santa Fe, which today has $42 billion in client assets.

Conservation

↵ **Dale Ball** (1923-2016) was a navigator in B-26 bombers in WWII. He was the owner of the Bank of Santa Fe and founder of the Santa Fe Conservation Trust. He completed the Dale Ball Trails at the age of 80 and lived in Santa Fe

↵ **Polly Mead Patraw** (1904-2001) was a botanist, the first female ranger-naturalist at Grand Canyon National Park, and the second ranger in the National Park Service. After her career, she retired to Santa Fe.

↵ **Ted Turner** (born 1938) is the largest private landowner in New Mexico, owning over one million acres. A true conservator of land, he has saved the Ladder Ranch, Armendaris Ranch, and the Vermejo Park Ranch. Being the largest landowner in New Mexico, I figure he's been to Santa Fe at least once, which must count for something.

Dance

↵ **Dana Tai Soon Burgess** (born 1968) is a dancer, choreographer, and Smithsonian's first Choreographer-in-Residence at the National Portrait Gallery. He graduated from Santa Fe High School and the University of New Mexico.

↵ **Martha Graham** (1894-1994) was an American dancer and choreographer who revolutionized the world of modern dance. She developed her own unique style of dance, characterized by angular, dramatic movements and emotional intensity. She rejected the traditional ballet techniques of the time and instead focused on expressing human emotions and experiences through movement. Her ashes are scattered across the Sangre de Cristo Mountain range above Santa Fe.

Fashion

⤸ **Perry Ellis** (1940-1986) was a fashion designer who designed the costumes for *Blithe Spirit*, a Noel Coward play, for The Santa Fe Festival Theatre in 1983.

⤸ **Tom Ford** (born 1961) is a fashion designer, writer, and director. He is often credited with saving Gucci when he was the creative director. He wrote and directed the films *A Single Man* (2009) and *Nocturnal Animals* (2016). He owned the 20,000-acre Cerro Pelon Ranch in Santa Fe, which sold for a reported $75 million. His father had a real estate company here in Santa Fe.

⤸ **Alexander Girard** (1907-1993) was director of Herman Miller textiles from 1952 to 73 and designed more than 300 innovative fabrics, some of which enhanced Charles and Ray Eames and George Nelson's furniture. In 1965, Braniff International hired him to make over its image and completely redesign each step of the airline passenger's experience. He had a collection of 106.000 pieces of folk art from all over the world, which he donated to the Museum of International Folk Art. Girard himself designed a new wing at the museum to house the collection.

⤸ **Lloyd Henry Kiva New** (1916-2002) was a designer and educator. He opened his boutique called Kiva in Scottsdale, Arizona, in 1945. He was the first Native American to show at an international fashion show when he was part of the Atlantic City International Fashion Show in 1951. In 1957, Miss Arizona Lynn Freyse wore a Kiva creation at the Miss America Pageant. In 1962, he co-founded the Institute of American Indian Arts (IAIA) as art director and later as director.

⤸ **Suzette Arpels Naumer,** also known as Suzette Arpels, was the daughter of Jacques Arpels, one of the founders of the jewelry company Van Cleef & Arpels. Suzette Arpels married Jack Naumer, an American diplomat. The couple settled in Santa Fe. She was known for her involvement in cultural and philanthropic activities in Santa Fe, especially the arts, and she had a shop, "Suzette's of La Fonda."

Legislation

⤸ **Fred Nathan, Jr.** founded "Think New Mexico" and is its Executive Director. He served as Special Counsel to New Mexico Attorney General Tom Udall from 1991-1998 when he was the architect of several successful legislative initiatives. He was also in charge of New Mexico's lawsuit against the tobacco industry, which resulted in a $1.25 billion settlement for the state. He serves on the boards of the New Mexico Foundation for Open Government, Santa Fe Preparatory School, and the Thornburg Foundation. He is a former trustee of his alma mater, Williams College. He lives in Santa Fe.

Movies and TV

- **Alan Arkin** (1934-2023) was an actor who won an Academy Award for *Little Miss Sunshine* and was nominated for an Emmy, a Golden Globe, and two Screen Actors Guild awards. He lived in Santa Fe for about 10 years.

- **Merrill Brockway** (1923–2013) was an Emmy Award-winning producer and director. He produced the PBS TV series *Dance in America* and the film version of George Balanchine's *The Nutcracker*. He retired to Santa Fe in 1993.

- **Carol Burnett** (born 1933) is an actress and comedian who hosted the *Carol Burnett Show* for 12 years. She lived in Santa Fe on an eight-acre compound on Circle Drive (7 bedrooms, 11 bathrooms, with a two-bedroom gatehouse and a two-bedroom casita). The house was on the cover of Architectural Digest's December 1996 issue.

- **Jordan Cronenweth** (1935-1996) was the director of photography for *Final Analysis* (1992), *Peggy Sue Got Married* (1986), and *Blade Runner* (1982). He owned a house in Tesuque.

- **Ted Danson**, (born 1947) played Sam Malone on the NBC sitcom *Cheers*, winning two Primetime Emmy Awards and two Golden Globe Awards. He was nominated for Emmy Awards for roles in the legal drama *Damages* (2007–2010) and the NBC dramedy *The Good Place* (2016–2020). He was awarded a star on Hollywood's Walk of Fame in 1999. He owned a house in Tesuque.

- **Brian Dennehy** (1938-2020) was an actor who won two Tony Awards, an Olivier Award, and a Golden Globe and received six Primetime Emmy Award nominations. Dennehy had roles in over 180 films and in many television and stage productions. He owned a home in Santa Fe.

⟡ **Greer Garson** (1904-1996) was an actress and philanthropist. She donated several million dollars for the construction of the Greer Garson Theater at both the Santa Fe University of Art and Design and SMU's Meadows School of the Arts on three conditions: 1) the stages must be circular, 2) the premier production must be *A Midsummer Night's Dream* and 3) must have large ladies' rooms. She and her husband, Buddy Fogelson, owned a ranch called Forked Lightning Ranch just outside Santa Fe. Garson and Fogelson were prominent figures in Santa Fe society during their time here, known for their philanthropy and contributions to the local community.

⟡ **Chris Eyre** (born 1968) is a director and producer who received Peabody and Emmy awards for his work as a filmmaker. He was chair of the film department at the Santa Fe University of Art and Design.

⟡ **Anna Gunn** (born 1968) is an actress who won the Primetime Emmy Award for Outstanding Supporting Actress in a Drama Series in 2013 and 2014 for playing Skyler White on *Breaking Bad*. She grew up in Santa Fe and graduated from Santa Fe Prep.

⟡ **Gene Hackman** (born 1930) won the Oscar for *The French Connection* and *Unforgiven* and was nominated for others. He is also the author of several novels. He has lived in Santa Fe since the 1980s, and his home was featured in Architectural Digest in 1990.

⟡ **Larry Hagman** (1931-2012) was a film and television actor, director, and producer best known for playing J. R. Ewing in the 1978–1991 primetime television soap opera *Dallas* and the astronaut Major Anthony Nelson in the 1965–1970 sitcom *I Dream of Jeannie*.

⟡ **Jack Handey** (born 1949) is an American humorist. He created "Deep Thoughts," which aired on The Comedy Channel (1989-1990) and Saturday Night Live (1991-1998). He and his wife, Marta Chavez, live in Santa Fe.

⟡ **Jim Henson** (1936-1990) was the creator of the Muppets. He owned 313 acres in Santa Fe.

⟡ **Martha Hyer** (1924-2014) was an actress in many movies, including *Some Came Running*, for which she was nominated for the Academy

Award for Best Supporting Actress. She also wrote the screenplay for Rooster Cogburn and was a long-time resident of Santa Fe.

♪ **Val Kilmer** (born 1954) is an actor who has appeared in *Top Gun* and *Willow* and played Jim Morrison in Oliver Stone's *The Doors*. His home in Tesuque appeared in the *April 1998 issue of Architectural Digest*.

♪ **Ali MacGraw** (born 1939) is an actress who may be best known for *Love Story* and *Goodbye Columbus* but has appeared in many others. Everyone my age was totally in love with her. She came to Santa Fe when her home in Malibu, California, burned to the ground. Her activism helped ban cockfighting in New Mexico, supported the permanent sanctuary of chimpanzees used in painful experiments, and advocated for stronger penalties for animal abusers and a ban on animal-killing contests.

She has embraced her life in Santa Fe and is often seen around the city. She is dedicated to women's, gay, and animal rights. She is active in Santa Fe, contributing to causes she believes in, and has become a valuable and vibrant part of the city.

♪ **Shirley MacLaine** (born 1934) was the Golden Globe winner in Alfred Hitchcock's *The Trouble With Harry*, Oscar winner for Best Actress in 1984 for *Terms of Endearment*, winner of Italian and German Oscars, three-time Emmy winner and ten-time Golden Globe winner. She has appeared in over fifty films, been nominated six times for Academy Awards, and is the author of nine international bestsellers. She is a long-time resident of Santa Fe with a pueblo-style home that sits on 4.7 acres and reflects her interest in metaphysics and higher consciousness. She actively advocates for women's issues, gay rights, and against animal cruelty. Her commitment to **spirituality** and **conscious living** perfectly resonates with Santa Fe.

♪ **Steve Martin** (Born 1945) is a comedian, actor, writer, producer, and musician. He has won five Grammy Awards, a Primetime Emmy Award, an Honorary Academy Award, and was nominated for two Tony Awards for his musical *Bright Star* in 2016. He lived in Santa Fe in the 1970s.

♪ **Lori Nelson** (1933-2020) was a movie actress who appeared in the TV series *How to Marry a Millionaire* and the films *Revenge of the Creature*, *All I Desire*, and *I Died a Thousand Times*. She was a long-time resident of Santa Fe.

- **Robert Redford** (born 1936) is an actor and director. He was named by *Time* as one of the 100 most influential people in the world in 2014. He lives on a 250-acre ranch outside Santa Fe.

- **Julia Roberts** (born 1967) is an actress who owned a home in Taos which she had bought from former Secretary of Defense Donald Rumsfeld. (OK, it's not Santa Fe, but it's close (kind of), and I like Julia Roberts).

- **Brad Sherwood** (born 1964) is an actor, singer, and comedian. He appeared in *Whose Line Is It Anyway* from 2014 to 2023. He grew up in Santa Fe.

- **Wes Studi** (born 1947) is a Native American actor, producer, and musician. He was inducted into the Oklahoma City Hall of Great Western Performers - Western Heritage Award. In 2019, he received an Honorary Academy Award, becoming the first Native American actor to receive an Oscar specifically for acting. He serves as honorary chair of the national endowment campaign of the Indigenous Language Institute in Santa Fe. He and his wife have a farm near Santa Fe.

- **Oprah Winfrey** (born 1954) was the richest African American in the 20th century and was once the world's only African American billionaire. She owned a house in Tesuque.

Music

- **Florence Birdwell** (1924–2021) is a musician and teacher. She taught musical theater and opera singing for more than six decades. She grew up in Santa Fe.

- **Melissa Etheridge** (born 1961) is a singer, songwriter, musician, and guitarist who owned a home in Santa Fe.

- **Jean Kraft** (1927–2021) was a mezzo-soprano opera singer. After retiring from opera in 1990, she divided her time between her family and teaching singing in Santa Fe. Her husband, the violinist Richard Elias, played in the Met Orchestra and retired with her. The couple built a house in Santa Fe in 1974, where they lived when not in New York City.

- **Peter Lieberson** (1946-2011) was a composer whose works were performed by the top U.S. orchestras and soloists, including cellist Yo-Yo Ma and pianists Emanuel Ax and Peter Serkin. He was a long-time resident of Santa Fe. He was the son of Goddard Lieberson, then president of Columbia Records, and Vera Zorina, an actress and former ballerina.

↵ **Katleen McIntosh** is a renowned harpsichordist who has established herself as a leading figure in the world of early keyboard music, particularly Baroque music. She has performed extensively as a soloist and chamber musician nationally and internationally. She is known for her sensitive and expressive interpretations of Baroque repertoire, often collaborating with leading period instrument ensembles and orchestras. McIntosh's performances are characterized by her mastery of the harpsichord, an instrument central to Baroque music. She is also a teacher and regularly travels to Havana, Lima, and Opole in Poland.

↵ **Wendy Rule** (born 1966) is an Australian-born musician with 11 studio albums and has toured the world extensively as a musician and educator in pagan spirituality. She lives in Santa Fe.

↵ **Randy Travis** *(born 1959) is a member of the* Country Music Hall of Fame and he has won seven Grammy Awards, 11 Academy of Country Music statuettes, 10 American Music Awards, two People's Choice awards, seven Music City News awards, eight Dove Awards from the Gospel Music Association, and five Country Music Association honors. He has also won three CMA Song of the Year with *On the Other Hand* (1986), *Forever and Ever Amen* (1987), and *Three Wooden Crosses* (2002). So far, he has 23 No. 1 singles, 31 Top-10, and has appeared in more than 40 feature films and television shows. *He owned an 8,750-square-foot adobe house here in Santa Fe.*

↵ **Pinchas Zukerman** (born 1948) is a violinist and conductor. His recordings have won 21 Grammy nominations and two Grammy wins. He had a house in Santa Fe when he was married to actress Tuesday Weld.

Newspapers

↵ **Robin Martin** (born 1954) is the owner of the Santa Fe New Mexican and the Taos News. She was inducted into the New Mexico Press Association Hall of Fame.

↵ **Richard McCord** (1941-2020) founded the Santa Fe Reporter in 1971 and wrote *The Chain Gang: One Newspaper Versus the Gannett Empire.*

Philanthropy

- **Andrew Davis** (born 1963) is a philanthropist, mutual fund manager, and the owner of the largest house in Santa Fe at over 26,000 square feet.

- **Anne Marion** (1938-2020) was a Texas rancher, oil heiress, and patron of the arts who founded the Georgia O'Keeffe Museum.

Poetry

- **Alice Corbin Henderson** (1881-1949) was a poet who first came to Santa Fe for tuberculosis treatment at Sunmount Sanitorium. She stayed to become an activist on behalf of the land and Native American civil rights. With her husband, the artist William Penhallow Henderson, she helped co-found the museum House of Navajo Religion (now the Wheelwright Museum of the American Indian) as well as the Eugene Manlove Rhodes Memorial Association. She published several volumes of poetry, including *The Linnet Songs* (1898), *The Spinning Woman of the Sky* (1912), *Red Earth: Poems of New Mexico* (1920), and *The Sun Turns West* (1933). She was an associate editor at *Poetry* from 1912 until 1922, and she co-edited, with Harriet Monroe, three editions of the anthology *The New Poetry* (1923 and 1932). Henderson also edited the New Mexican poetry anthologies *The Turquoise Trail* (1928) and *New Mexico: A Guide to the Colorful State* (1937).

Politics

- **Charles Bent** (1799-1847) was the first civilian US Governor of the New Mexico Territory. He married Maria Ignacia Jaramillo, born in Taos. Her younger sister, Josefa, married Kit Carson.

- **Thomas Benton Catron** (1840-1921) was a controversial politician. The good: He was a US Senator who pushed for New Mexico statehood. The bad: He was against women's suffrage and the leader of the Santa Fe Ring. As a lawyer familiar with Mexican land grants, Catron gained an interest in or clear title to 34 grants totaling 3,000,000 acres. By 1894, he was the largest landowner in the United States.

- **Bronson M. Cutting** (1888–1935) was a US Senator from New Mexico, and he published the *Santa Fe New Mexican* and *El Nuevo Mexicano*. He served in the US Senate from 1927 until he died in a plane crash in 1935. He first came to Santa Fe in 1910 to recover from tuberculosis at Sunmount Sanatorium. He and his sister had a home on Old Santa Fe Trail, called Los Siete Burros (The Seven Burros).

ᶌ **John Eastman** (born 1960) is a lawyer and academic who has been criminally indicted in Georgia and recommended for disbarment in California for his role in attempting to keep then-president Donald Trump in office after his election defeat in 2020. He has been a resident of Santa Fe.

ᶌ **George and Javier Gonzalez** were father and son mayors of Santa Fe. Father George was mayor from 1968-1972 and son Javier was mayor from 2014-2018.

ᶌ **Debby Jamarillo** (born 1952) was mayor of Santa Fe and promised to place the interests of local residents above those of Santa Fe's tourist industry.

ᶌ **Sam Pick** (Born 1936) was twice mayor of Santa Fe and a pro-business promoter of Santa Fe.

ᶌ **Arthur Seligman** (1871-1933) was Santa Fe's Mayor and New Mexico's Governor.

ᶌ **Lew Wallace** (1827–1905) was the New Mexico Territorial Governor from 1878 to 1881. He was a lawyer, Civil War Union general, politician, US Minister to the Ottoman Empire, artist, and, not least, author of Ben-Hur, the best-selling American novel of the 19th century. He lived in Santa Fe while he was governor.

Political Cartoonist

ᶌ **Pat Oliphant** (Born 1935) is a Pulitzer Prize-winning political cartoonist whose work has been syndicated internationally since 1965. He has produced thousands of daily editorial cartoons, bronze sculptures, drawings, and paintings that have left their mark on the world of art and political commentary. His works are held in the permanent collections of the Library of Congress, the National Portrait Gallery, the Gerald R. Ford Presidential Museum, the George W. Bush Library, The University of Colorado Library, and our own New Mexico Museum of Art. He retired in 2015 and lives in Santa Fe with his wife, Susan Conway Oliphant.

Religious

⤵ **Mother Magdalene and the Sisters of Loretto** (1852-1968) included Mother Magdalen Hayden and Sisters Roberta Brown, Rosana Dant, and Catherine Mahoney, who arrived in Santa Fe from Kentucky in 1852. In 1853, they established Our Lady of Light Academy, later known as Loretto, which became the first school for young women in the Territory of New Mexico. The Sisters of Loretto played a pivotal role in education, culture, and community life in Santa Fe and beyond. Between 1863 and 1879, the Sisters raised funds to build the Loretto Chapel.

Science

⤵ **George Cowan** (1920-2012) was a physical chemist who worked on the Manhattan Project, one of the founders of the Santa Fe Opera, and one of the founders and first president of the Santa Fe Institute.

⤵ **Murray Gell Mann** (1929-2019) was a physicist who won the Nobel Prize and was one of the founders of the Santa Fe Institute, where he held the title of Distinguished Fellow. He coined the word "quark." He lived in Santa Fe.

⤵ **Dorothy McKibbin** (1897–1985) ran the Manhattan Project's office at 109 East Palace Avenue, for which she was known as the "Gatekeeper of Los Alamos." According to the author, Jennet Conant, in 109 East Palace, she never knew and never asked what the purpose of Los Alamos was. She lived in Santa Fe from 1932 on. Her son was the head park ranger at Bandelier National Monument.

⤵ **Stanislaw Ulam** (1909–1984) was a mathematician associated with the Manhattan Project. In 1980, Ulam and his wife appeared in the television documentary *The Day After Trinity*. In 1947, he proposed a statistical approach to the problem of neutron diffusion in fissionable material, which became the "Monte Carlo Method." He kept a residence in Santa Fe for consulting in Los Alamos.

Service

⤵ **Laura Liswood**, a lawyer, started out as manager of TWA's Charter Operations and ended up working in global leadership and diversity for

Goldman Sachs. After 911, she felt she needed to do something, so she became the oldest female bicycle cop with the DC Metropolitan Police Force eventually making sergeant in the Special Operations Division. Prior to that, she interviewed every democratically elected female head of state and government in the world which became a documentary shown on NPR. She and the president of Iceland founded the Council of Women World Leaders to bring together past and present female leaders each year, giving them the unique opportunity to talk with their peers. She has written The Loudest Duck and The Elephant and the Mouse about diversity, Serving Them Right, and Women World Leaders about the interviews with the women leaders. She has also bicycled across Siberia and the Silk Route. She was a long-time resident of Bethesda, Maryland, but now lives in Santa Fe.

*   **Peter Ives** is president of Ives Enterprises, Inc. After moving to Santa Fe in 1983, Peter was in private practice for about 15 years, then became in-house counsel for The Trust for Public Land and served as General Counsel for the New Mexico Department of Cultural Affairs, retiring in December 2022. Along the way, he served two terms as Santa Fe city councilor and was Mayor Pro Tem under Mayor Javier Gonzales. He graduated from Harvard and Georgetown University Law Center. He currently sits on a half dozen non-profit boards, and at the City, is the citizen alternate member of the Buckman Direct Diversion Board, is on Santa Fe's Sister Cities Committee, continues volunteer work for the UNESCO Creative Cities organization, and serves on the Santa Fe Food Policy Council. Peter is also working on creating more attainable workforce housing in Santa Fe. He and his wife are longtime residents of Santa Fe.

*   **Abe and Marion Silver.** This amazing couple served on nearly every service organization in Santa Fe. They owned the apparel store, "The Guarantee on the Plaza."

Social

*   **Claude James** founded Claude's Bar on Canyon Road in 1955. It was the first gay bar in Santa Fe and the center of social life, attracting every colorful character in Santa Fe. It was raucous, rowdy, fun, and legendary.

By the way, Claude was a she. Claude's Bar is now the Silver Sun Gallery.

Sports

✒ **Don Meredith** (1938-2010), AKA "Dandy Don," was a quarterback for the Dallas Cowboys, commentator for Monday Night Sports with Howard Cosell and Frank Gifford, and an actor, appearing in many TV shows and films, including *Police Story* and *Mayday at 40,000 Feet!* He lived in Santa Fe. His daughter still lives here.

Technology

✒ **Paul Allen** (1953-2018) was co-founder of Microsoft Corporation who gave away over $2 billion as a philanthropist to education, wildlife, environmental conservation, the arts, and healthcare. He bought Georgia O'Keeffe's estate (Sol Y Sombra) on Old Santa Fe Trail (18,663 square feet, 21 bedrooms, 26 bathrooms, and 20 acres) which he owned from 2000 until his death.

Born in Santa Fe

✒ **Manuel de Sandoval** (estimated 1680s -1740s) was the colonial Governor of Texas. He was the only native of New Mexico who governed Spanish Texas.

✒ **Donaciano Vigil**, (1802-1877). Territorial Governor of New Mexico

✒ **Raoul Trujillo** (born 1955) is a dancer, choreographer, and movie actor who is the original choreographer and co-director of the American Indian Dance Theatre, but he might be best known for playing Zero Wolf in Mel Gibson's *Apocalypto* (2006).

✒ **Debbie Martinez** (1959-2019), "La Chicanita", was a singer.

✒ **Adrian Grenier** (born 1976) is a TV actor best known for his portrayal of Vincent Chase in the television series *Entourage* and has appeared in films such as *Drive Me Crazy, The Devil Wears Prada, Trash Fire*, and *Marauders.*

✒ **Josh West** (born 1977), Olympic medalist rower and Earth Sciences professor. He graduated from Yale and Cambridge.

♪ **Jeremy Ray Valdez,** (born 1980). Actor, writer, and producer. Received the 2010 Imogen Award for Best Supporting Actor in *La Mission* with Benjamin Bratt.

♪ **America Young** (born 1984) is a TV actress is an actress and director, known for *Girls! Girls! Girls!* (2011), *The Concessionaires Must Die!* (2017) and *Electoral Emissions* (2012).

♪ **Aviva Baumann,** actress best known for her role as Nikola in the comedy, *Superbad* (born 1984).

♪ **Teal Swan** (born 1984) is an author, spiritual leader, bestselling author, and artist. She was the subject of the 2017 documentary film *Open Shadow: The Story of Teal Swan.*

♪ **Charlotte Fox** (born 1985) is an actress known for being in *Devil Wears a Suit* (2017), *Love & Other Emotions* (2013), and *Jilted* (2015).

♪ **Zach Condon** (born 1986) is a folk singer, lead singer, and songwriter of the band "Beirut."

Chapter 5

A LITTLE HISTORY

STRANGE CONNECTIONS THAT SHAPED SANTA FE

Who Knew?

The Spanish Inquisition

The Spanish Inquisition had a significant impact on Santa Fe's history. Centuries before New Mexico became a U.S. state, it was part of the Spanish Empire. During this time, Sephardic Jews (Jews of Spain) faced persecution due to the Alhambra Decree of 1492, signed by King Ferdinand and Queen Isabella, banishing all Jews in Spain. They had the option to convert to Catholicism or leave the country. In 1497, the king of Portugal also forced Jews in Portugal to leave the country or convert.

The Jews who stayed in Spain and converted were called *conversos, while the Jews who practiced* their Jewish faith in secret were the *crypto-Jews* (secret Jews). When the Spanish Catholic Church started the Holy Office of the Inquisition, the crypto-Jews began to be persecuted because while the Inquisition had no authority over Jews, it did over Catholics, so the crypto-Jews were targeted.

The same year that Queen Isabella banned Jews from Spain, Christopher Columbus "discovered" the New World. After that, thousands of crypto-Jew immigrants settled in American colonies to live as Catholics but practiced Judaism in secret.

The Inquisition eventually came to the Spanish colonies in America, with campaigns against Mexican crypto-Jews in the sixteenth and seventeenth centuries. These campaigns pushed them to migrate to New Mexico, the far northern border of Spanish colonial territory. There, they continued to practice their Jewish customs in secret, attempting to blend into the region's mostly Catholic culture.

In New Mexico today, there are still signs that this crypto-Jewish heritage is alive in the Hispanic community. Because crypto Jews came to New Mexico hundreds of years and many generations ago, some families today don't realize they are practicing parts of the Jewish faith, such as lighting candles on Friday night, observing the Sabbath on Saturday, or not eating pork products but others have deliberately passed down the Jewish traditions through the generations.

Tuberculosis

Tuberculosis played a significant role in Santa Fe's history. From the late 19th century until the 1940s, it was the leading cause of death in the United States. Before antibiotics, the primary treatment for tuberculosis patients involved fresh air, lots of sunshine, low humidity, and high altitude, which Santa Fe had in abundance.

As a result, sanatoriums opened across the state, becoming the basis for New Mexico's modern health care system. For example, Presbyterian Hospital, Christus St. Vincent's Hospital in Santa Fe, and The Lovelace hospitals in Albuquerque started as Lovelace Sanatorium, run by Dr. Lovelace.

Sunmount began in 1880 as a collection of tent houses and small cottages. Later, in the early 20th century, Dr. Frank Meara and his wife established a hospital there.

Many who came seeking treatment found healing and stayed in Santa Fe, contributing significantly to Santa Fe. Among them were:

- Carlos Vierra: An artist who advocated for the Pueblo Revival architectural style and recovered in Santa Fe.

- John Gaw Meem: An architect who contracted tuberculosis while working on the New York City subway system. He later settled in Santa Fe and designed buildings like the Cristo Rey church.

- Will Shuster: The Santa Fe artist who created Zozobra sought a cure after suffering from mustard gas poisoning during World War I.

- New Mexico U.S. Senators Clinton P. Anderson and Bronson Cutting: Both came to the state while suffering from tuberculosis.

- Dr. William Randolph Lovelace: A physician from Missouri who arrived in New Mexico with tuberculosis. His name is now on one of the major hospitals in the state.

⚜ Poet Alice Corbin Henderson

Primogeniture & Spanish Aristocracy

The definition of Primogeniture is that the eldest son inherits the family's wealth and property, not split between the children. This practice has existed in Spain since the 11th Century and is deeply rooted in European tradition. So, if you were the second or third son (daughters were not in the mix), you were out of luck.

So, what would you do if you were an aristocrat in Spain with no hope and no prospects? One possibility was to seek your fortune by going to the New World. Spanish nobility, because of primogeniture, played a significant role in conquering the New World. They sought riches, land, and titles in the Americas since they could not get them in Spain.

Primogeniture shaped the European aristocracy's decisions to go beyond Spain, contributing to the exploration, colonization, and establishment of European presence in the Americas. Explorers and conquistadors were both key figures in the Age of Exploration, but they had different goals and methods. Explorers were primarily interested in discovering new lands, mapping coastlines, and establishing trade routes. They were often sponsored by monarchs or trading companies and were focused on scientific discovery, trade, and cultural exchange.

Conquistadors, on the other hand, were Spanish soldiers and adventurers, many of Spanish nobility who sought to conquer and colonize new territories, particularly in the Americas, to find gold, expand the Spanish Empire, and spread Christianity. This often resulted in violent conflicts with indigenous peoples to establish colonial rule.

Why is there a Hebrew inscription on the entrance to the Cathedral Basilica of St. Francis of Assisi?

Archbishop Jean Baptiste Lamy was lacking in funds to finish the construction of the Cathedral Basilica of St. Francis of Assisi, so he sought financial help from Santa Fe's Jewish merchants to complete the church. The Jewish community responded with contributions, and the Cathedral was able to be completed. Acknowledgment of this help appears above the doors of the main entrance; as you enter, if you look up, you can see a triangle at the top of the arch, an inscription in the ancient Hebrew Tetragram of YHWH (the name of God in the Hebrew bible).

Flamenco in Santa Fe?
YES!

Flamenco is intimately connected with the broader cultural and historical influences that have shaped Santa Fe.

- Spanish Colonial Influence: Flamenco traces its origins to Andalusia, Spain, and reflects a blend of Romani, Moorish, and Spanish cultures. During the Spanish colonial period in New Mexico, which began in the 16th century, Spanish settlers brought their cultural traditions, including music and dance, to Santa Fe.

- Early 20th Century: In the early 20th century, there was increased interest in Spanish and Mexican arts across the United States. This period saw the establishment of cultural societies and artistic communities dedicated to preserving and promoting Spanish traditions, including flamenco. In Santa Fe, this cultural revival contributed to the development of a local interest in flamenco.

- Cultural Institutions and Festivals: Over time, Santa Fe became known for its cultural institutions and festivals that celebrate a wide range of arts, including flamenco. These events provide platforms for flamenco artists to showcase their talents and educate audiences about the art form's rich history and significance.

- Continued Appreciation and Growth: Today, flamenco continues to thrive in Santa Fe, supported by a community of artists, educators, and enthusiasts.

Several individuals have made significant contributions to the local flamenco scene, helping its popularity over the years.

- Maria Benitez was born to a Native American mother and a Puerto Rican father. She studied and performed in Spain during the 1960s and later founded the Institute for Spanish Arts and Teatro Flamenco, which was a regular part of the cultural scene in Santa Fe for decades. After retiring, she continued teaching at the Institute and disbanded Teatro Flamenco in 2007.

- La Emi, a New Mexico native, is a well-known performer and teacher. She began studying Flamenco with the María Benítez Institute for

Spanish Arts (ISA) at the age of four. In 2014, she founded her own dance company, EmiArteFlamenco, and in 2017, she founded both EmiArteFlamenco Academy, a school for students of all ages, and Flamenco Youth de Santa Fe, a children's company that performs for communities all around New Mexico.

- Marisol Encinias: Marisol Encinias, daughter of Eva Encinias-Sandoval, is a flamenco dancer and teacher who has performed and taught extensively in New Mexico, including Santa Fe. Her contributions to flamenco education and performance have inspired a new generation of flamenco enthusiasts and practitioners.

- Antonio Granjero is a flamenco dancer and choreographer who has performed worldwide and settled in Santa Fe. He co-founded the Institute for Spanish Arts in Santa Fe, which promoted Spanish arts and culture, with a particular emphasis on flamenco. Granjero's contributions to the local flamenco community include performances, workshops, and educational outreach programs.

- Vicente Romero (1937-1995) is often credited with creating the vibrant flamenco scene in northern New Mexico.

- Yjastros: The American Flamenco Repertory Company: Although based primarily in Albuquerque, Yjastros is the oldest professional flamenco company in the United States with a significant presence in New Mexico, including performances and collaborations in Santa Fe. Yjastros has contributed to the visibility and appreciation of flamenco across the state, influencing the local flamenco scene in Santa Fe through performances and educational initiatives.

Some places where you can see flamenco in Santa Fe:

- Maria Benitez Cabaret at The Lodge features regular performances by professional flamenco dancers.

- La Boca is a tapas restaurant that occasionally features flamenco performances.

- El Farol offers authentic Spanish cuisine and drinks and regularly features flamenco shows accompanied by Spanish guitar music and sometimes singing.

- El Flamenco de Santa Fe: This dedicated flamenco venue hosts performances by local and visiting flamenco artists. It offers a variety of shows, ranging from traditional flamenco to innovative contemporary interpretations.

𝓈 Inn and Spa at Loretto occasionally hosts flamenco performances.

𝓈 Santa Fe Bandstand: During the Santa Fe Fiesta, the Plaza Gazebo is the venue for free outdoor concerts and performances, including flamenco dancing. This event series showcases a diverse range of musical and dance performances, including flamenco.

𝓈 Santa Fe Fiesta Market occurs during the annual Santa Fe Fiesta, which is held in September and features live entertainment, including flamenco dancers.

FYI: I know you know this:
Flamenco is from Spain. Tango is from Argentina.

A Brief History

Historically, three different peoples and their cultures have had major influences on making Santa Fe what it is today: Pueblo, Spanish, and Anglo.

The Pueblo People actually got their name from the Spanish, with Pueblo being the Spanish word for 'village.' The Pueblo People called themselves simply "The People." Each Pueblo is completely independent from the others, with different forms of governing. Within the 19 Pueblos, there are five languages.

Almost all the Pueblo societies are matrilineal, meaning that the women own the property and pass it to their daughters. Women may run the family, but the men govern the pueblo, including the ceremonies. The Pueblo religion is nature-oriented, working to live in harmony with nature. Kachina dolls could represent the spirits of a tree, bird, fish, place, or rock. The Pueblo People have dances that show respect for the aspects of nature that provide for their life, such as good crops and productive hunts.

The Spanish conquistadors in the New World had two purposes: the first was to convert the natives to Christianity, and the second was to find wealth for the King of Spain. These were the "Twin Majesties": God in heaven and the King of Spain on earth.

In 1598, Don Juan de Onate launched the first colonizing expedition. He established the capital at San Juan Pueblo, about 25 miles north of Santa Fe. From there, the Franciscans built 50 churches between 1600-1625 to convert the Pueblos. Don Pedro de Peralta, the third governor of New Mexico, moved the capital to Santa Fe to be more central to the Pueblos, had better access to water, and could better be defended from the Native Americans. The first 70 years of Spanish rule were violent, finally resulting in the Pueblo Revolt of 1680, which forced the Spaniards back into Mexico. But this was only temporary, for in 1692-93, Don Diego de Vargas reconquered Santa Fe to put it back into Spanish control.

Until the early 19th century, Spain allowed no foreign trade, so Santa Fe and New Mexico were isolated. It took the Louisiana Purchase in 1803 to get the momentum to push west, ignoring Spain's restrictions. Another factor was Spain's preoccupation with the Napoleonic wars in Europe, with Spain losing its grip on Mexico. Mexico was able to gain independence from Spain in 1821.

Despite Spain's efforts to keep outsiders from entering, an explorer named Zebulon Pike came to Santa Fe in 1807. He was promptly taken prisoner and hustled to Chihuahua, Mexico. After he was released, he published his travel journals and BANG! New Mexico was no longer unknown in the United States. Then, with the opening of the Santa Fe Trail in 1822, traders flocked to the territory that was ripe to being developed. In 1850, New Mexico became a territory of the United States and a territory it remained until becoming a state in 1912. The first Anglo settlers of the 19th century were largely merchants and traders who stayed to establish businesses together with homesteaders, cattle ranchers, and the adventuresome. In the 1920s, this changed. The Santa Fe art colony blossomed with Santa Fe's relaxed atmosphere, terrific colors, and high and dry climate.

Jewish Merchants of Santa Fe

Jewish merchants have contributed to Santa Fe's economic growth and influenced its art, culture, and community life. Some notable examples:

Solomon Spiegelberg arrived in Santa Fe in 1846, becoming the first Jewish merchant on the Santa Fe Trail. Like the crypto-Jews who fled in the 15th and 16th centuries, Spiegelberg came to the New World in the 19th century to escape oppression in his homeland. Being a businessman, he saw the growing commercial needs of the West after the Mexican-American War. In 1846, he set up a small mercantile business in Santa Fe. Solomon's younger brothers followed him and, in 1848, formed the Spiegelberg Brothers Partnership. The store, located on the south side of the plaza across from the Governor's Palace, offered groceries and dry goods.

Abraham Staab established the first major economic empire in the territory. He originally worked for Solomon Spiegelberg but soon formed his own merchandise company with his brother Zadoc, becoming the largest wholesale distributor in the entire territory, making them some of the wealthiest and most influential men in the American Southwest. According to the La Posada website, at the height of its prosperity, the two brothers were earning a collective annual revenue of $600,000, which is more than $14 million in today's money. Abraham built the Staab Mansion for his wife Julia. The Staab House is now the La Posada de Santa Fe Hotel.

Other notable early Jewish merchants were the Wise family and the Grunsfeld family, who interestingly, had sons who married daughters of Solomon Spiegelberg.

The Penitentes

The Penitentes, also known as Los Hermanos Penitentes, are a religious brotherhood with deep roots in the cultural history of New Mexico. The Penitentes trace their origins to the early 19th century, when in 1822, following the Mexican independence from Spain, all priests from Spain were recalled to Spain (or thrown out, depending on your point of view). Since the vast majority of priests were Spanish, this left few to no priests, especially in rural areas of New Mexico. Since people still died, gave birth, got sick, and got married, there was a void. The Penitentes filled the void as best they could since they were just lay people.

When Bishop Jean-Baptiste Lamy arrived with French clergy, the Penitentes were excommunicated because they were not real priests. This did not endear them to the bishop, but it also did not stop them. They continued in secret to blend Spanish Catholicism, pious customs, and unique rituals. The Penitentes are still active today. During Holy Week, the Penitentes lead solemn processions and perform flagellation as an act of penance.

Sunmount Sanatorium

Sunmount Sanitorium played a crucial role in the fight against tuberculosis from 1906 to 1937, when tuberculosis was the leading cause of death in the United States.

Sunmount Sanitorium began in 1880 as a series of tent cottages in Santa Fe. People suffering from the disease sought refuge in the high desert mountains of New Mexico, hoping to find a cure. The primary treatment for tuberculosis before antibiotics involved pristine air, sunshine, low humidity, and high altitude, which, of course, Santa Fe had.

In the early 20th century, Dr. Frank Mera and his wife established a hospital at Sunmount to care for those with tuberculosis. Sunmount Sanitorium not only provided medical care but also encouraged art and culture. Once cured, many remained in New Mexico, contributing significantly to the vitality of Santa Fe. Today, the Immaculate Heart of Mary Retreat and Conference Center stands where Sunmount once operated. The Archdiocese of Santa Fe recently sold it.

Santa Fe River

The Santa Fe River is 46 miles long and starts in the Sangre de Cristo Mountain range. In 2007, it was listed as one of the ten most endangered rivers in the United States. Historically, the Pueblo villages used the Santa Fe River to irrigate their fields. The Diné referred to the Santa Fe River as "Yootó," meaning "a string of water beads," describing the shallow pools of standing water along the river's course.

The Santa Fe Plaza

The Santa Fe Plaza is a National Historic Landmark that is the home to the Palace of the Governors, the oldest public building in the United States. The Plaza was founded by the Spanish in 1609 as a strategic location for defense and later served as the end of the Santa Fe Trail after Mexico gained its independence. When Anglo-Americans arrived around 1850, they enlarged the Plaza to about one city block and enclosed it with buildings facing the Palace of the Governors. While the surrounding buildings have changed over the years, the Plaza itself remains relatively unchanged. The Santa Fe Plaza was designated a National Landmark in 1960 and added to the National Register of Historic Places in 1966.

Fort Marcy

Fort Marcy is the only fort from the Mexican-American War that still exists in the United States.

It was built in 1846 by General Stephen W. Kearny during the Mexican-American War to house 280 men. It is located on a hill overlooking Santa Fe that is 50 yards higher and just 600 yards north of the Santa Fe Plaza. It had 14 cannons that could oppose a Mexican army or put down a local rebellion. Its adobe walls were nine feet tall and five feet thick forming Fort

Marcy's unique star-shaped outline.

The fort had a moat about eight feet deep around the fort and a log powder house. Today, only a few tall mounds of earth are visible where the walls used to be, and the moat is just about gone completely.

General Kearny played a little politics when he named the fort after the U.S. Secretary of War, William L. Marcy, who just happened to be his boss.

Lieutenant William H. Emory stated that the fort's site was "the only point which commands the entire town and which itself is commanded by no other." Fort Marcy saw little action during the American Civil War and was abandoned when President Andrew Johnson signed an executive order on August 28, 1868.

The New Mexico School for the Deaf

The New Mexico School for the Deaf was the first public school in New Mexico and is the only land-grant school for the deaf in the United States. It was founded privately in 1885 by Lars and Belle Larson, but the New Mexico legislature took it over in 1887. It provides education for deaf and hard-of-hearing students from preschool through grade 12. It can board as many as 96 students with a total student population of 142, a 79% minority student enrollment with 42% females and 58% males, and a student-teacher ratio of 4:1. There are 38 full-time equivalent teachers and 4 full-time school counselors. It serves every county in New Mexico and has a 100% graduation rate.

The Santa Fe Trail

This was primarily a trade route beginning in Franklin, Missouri, and ending in Santa Fe. It passed through Franklin, Missouri; Independence, Missouri; Council Grove, Kansas; Fort Larned, Kansas; Fort Dodge (Dodge City), Kansas; and Lakin, Kansas. The Trail started in 1821 and was in use until the railroad reached Santa Fe in 1880. According to the National Park Service, it would take somewhere between 8 to 10 weeks to travel the 869 miles.

Santa Fe Plaza Santa Fe Trail Monument is in front of the Palace of Governors and marks the end of the Santa Fe Trail. It is made of Salida, Colorado grey granite and was placed by the Daughters of the American Revolution in 1910.

Lowriders: Life in the Low Lane

A lowrider or low rider is a customized car with a lowered body that became popular with Mexican American youth in the late 1940s to early 1950s. They are not just about transportation but are rolling artworks often painted with intricate, colorful designs and featuring unique artistic elements. In the 1950s, many young white men loved hot rods and worked to make them as fast as possible. Traditional hotrods did not appeal to the young Mexican American men from southern California, Texas, and New Mexico. Unlike the "hot and fast" hot rods, they wanted "low and slow" automobiles. Instead of spending money on bigger, faster engines, they spent their money on appearance and style, eventually becoming the "lowrider."

Lowriders became so popular because they were fairly reasonable to make, only requiring a used, late-model car; the bigger, the better. Having a low cost was vitally important for the historically disadvantaged Hispanic communities.

With low and slow, the goal is style, not speed, and once you've got style, why go fast? Lowriders want to be seen as long as possible, so slow is way better than fast, leading to the lowrider's distinctive, long, and low look. At first, the easiest and cheapest way to get low was to put sandbags in the trunk. But later, they cut springs and used smaller diameter wheels, lower profile tires, and pneumatic lifts.

Once they lowered their cars, lowrider owners had a problem. They found that having really low cars was a magnet for police to pull them over. Not good. So, they installed hydraulic suspensions to raise their cars to be legal around police but could be lowered back down when the police were gone.

Interesting note 1: Española, just 24 miles away, has declared itself the "lowrider capital of the world."

Interesting note 2: Many lowriders first used (and still use) hydraulics from WWII and later airplanes that once controlled bomb doors, landing gear, and braking systems. For example, as the 744 B-52s built became surplus, they helped supply lowriders.

Adobe

Adobe bricks have traditionally been made by packing a mixture of mud, sand, and straw into a wooden frame and drying it in the sun. Stones are set in adobe mortar to provide a foundation for the bricks, and the dried bricks are then laid in adobe mortar to form exterior and interior walls.

The Adobe Factory, founded by Mel Medina in 1978 between Santa Fe and Taos, is the largest producer of adobe bricks in the state. It can manufacture 20,000 premium-quality products per day.

Palace of the Governors

Don Pedro de Peralta was appointed the new Governor of New Mexico in 1608 but he didn't arrive in New Mexico until 1610. He was ordered to create the Villa de Santa Fe as the capital of the province. The town was established on the north bank of the Santa Fe River. The town plaza and primary streets had been laid out when the settlement was originally established. The site for the town church was situated at the east end of the plaza, and the north side was selected for the governor's residence.

Note: New Mexico State Historian Rick Hendricks discovered in 2011 that it may have been constructed about 1618, not 1610 by a different governor.

La Fonda on the Plaza

There has probably been an inn of some kind at La Fonda's location since the 1600s. In 1846 when the US annexed New Mexico, the inn became the U.S. Hotel. Then, in the late 19th century, the U.S. Hotel became the Exchange Hotel. Today's La Fonda Hotel was constructed in 1922, replacing the Exchange Hotel at the same location. In 1925, the Atchison, Topeka, and Santa Fe Railway acquired the La Fonda Hotel and leased it to Fred Harvey. The La Fonda Hotel underwent its first expansion in 1927, adopting the distinctive Pueblo Revival architectural style. For over 40 years, from 1926 to 1968, it was one of the Harvey Houses, a prestigious chain of upscale hotels. The La Fonda Hotel itself was known for its unique blend of Southwestern charm, great food, and excellent service.

Harvey Houses

The Fred Harvey Company was founded in 1876 by Fred Harvey who owned a chain of restaurants, hotels, and other hospitality businesses alongside railroads in the Western United States to cater to the growing number of train passengers.

Fred Harvey, a former railroad freight agent, recognized the potential of providing higher-quality food and service at railroad eating establishments.

The Atchison, Topeka & Santa Fe Railway (AT&SF) contracted with Harvey for what would become several "Harvey Houses." The first Harvey House dining house-hotel establishment officially opened along the AT&SF

tracks in Florence, Kansas in 1878.

Harvey Houses became known for good food, customer service, fair treatment of employees, and preservation of local traditions. The company operated 84 Harvey House facilities throughout the West. Fred Harvey is credited with creating the first restaurant chain in the U.S. which played a significant role in promoting tourism in the Southwest during the late 19th century.

Harvey Girls

Harvey Girls were female employees of the Fred Harvey Company's nationwide chain. They were between the ages of 18-20 and of 'good character'. They had to sign a contract agreeing to stay on the job and not marry for one year. Harvey Girls were housed in dormitories and watched over by a housemother. They were recruited with the promise of adventure and good wages, and it worked. Young women from the East and Midwest made their way West to restaurants and hotels like our own La Fonda, providing guests with great service and food.

LGBTQ+

While the gay scene in Santa Fe is not large, it is inclusive, with cultural offerings and supportive organizations, making it comfortable for LGBTQ+ individuals and visitors.

- Community Organizations: Santa Fe is home to several LGBTQ+ community organizations that provide support, advocacy, and social activities, including the Santa Fe Human Rights Alliance, which promotes equality and provides resources for LGBTQ+ individuals.

- Nightlife: While not like larger cities, Santa Fe does have a few clubs that cater to the LGBTQ+ community. These establishments often host events and drag shows and provide spaces for socializing and networking.

- Events and Festivals: The city hosts various LGBTQ+ events and festivals throughout the year. One notable event is the annual Santa Fe Pride celebration, which includes a parade, performances, and community gatherings to celebrate diversity and promote LGBTQ+ visibility.

- Art and Culture: Santa Fe's artistic and cultural scene includes LGBTQ+ artists and events. Galleries, theaters, and cultural centers often showcase works and performances that explore LGBTQ+ themes and perspectives.

⤳ Inclusivity and Acceptance: Santa Fe prides itself on its inclusivity and acceptance, which is reflected in local policies and attitudes towards LGBTQ+ residents. The city government and community organizations actively work to ensure equal rights and opportunities for all residents.

The history of gay rights in Santa Fe is characterized by gradual progress toward equality. Here are some key milestones:

1. Early Activism: Like many places in the U.S., Santa Fe saw early activism centered around gay rights in the 1970s and 1980s. Activists worked to raise awareness, combat discrimination, and build community support.

2. Legal Advances:
- 1993: New Mexico becomes one of the first states to enact a hate crimes law that includes sexual orientation.

- 2003: The New Mexico Supreme Court rules in favor of adoption rights for same-sex couples, a significant step towards recognizing parental rights.

3. Marriage Equality:
- 2013: The New Mexico Supreme Court ruled in Griego v. Oliver that same-sex marriage is legal in the state, making it one of the earlier states to legalize same-sex marriage through judicial action.

4. Local Initiatives:
- Santa Fe has been supportive of LGBTQ+ rights at the local level, with city officials often advocating for inclusivity and nondiscrimination policies.

Santa Fe hosts a variety of events celebrating the LGBTQ+ community throughout the year.

1. Santa Fe Pride: Organized by the Human Rights Alliance, Santa Fe Pride is a major event featuring a parade, float competition, and various festivities. The parade kicks off from the Lamy Building parking lot and proceeds through historic parts of the city, ending at Marcy Street.

2. Pride Week Kickoff: The Pride Week Kick-Off T-Dance and Lawn Party take place at The Mystic Santa Fe.

3. Pride Drag Bingo: Hosted at Tumbleroot Brewery and Distillery,

Pride Drag Bingo is a fun and interactive event that combines bingo with the flair of drag performances.

4. Pride Bar Crawl offers a chance to explore the city's nightlife while celebrating Pride. Participants visit multiple bars and enjoy special events and drinks along the way.

5. Pride Movie Night: The New Mexico History Museum hosts a screening of "Word is Out: Stories of Some of Our Lives," a significant film documenting the lives and experiences of LGBTQ+ individuals.

National Historic Landmarks

Barrio De Analco Historic District includes the oldest house in the state and the oldest Catholic church in the continental United States.

El Santuario de Chimayo is famous for its history and as a contemporary pilgrimage site.

Glorieta Pass Battlefield is the site of the Civil War "Battle of Glorieta Pass.

Santa Fe Plaza became a National Historic Landmark in 1960.

Seton Village is a National Historic Landmark and a New Mexico State Cultural Property. It includes a residential settlement and educational facility established in 1930 by Ernest Thompson Seton (1860-1946), an educator and conservationist who founded the Woodcraft Indians in 1902 before the Boy Scouts of America started. In fact, Robert Baden-Powell, the founder of the Boy Scouts, used elements of the Woodcraft Indians.

National Park Service Region III Office is a great example of Spanish/Pueblo revival architecture. The building, known as one of the largest secular adobe buildings in the United States, was built between 1936 and 1939 by the Civilian Conservation Corps. It is listed on the National Register of Historic Places and National Historic Landmarks and designated as "Must-Be Preserved."

The Palace of the Governors is the oldest governmental building still in use in the United States and was built with three-foot-thick adobe walls for defense. From 1610-1907, it served as the official headquarters under four governments: The Kingdom of Spain (1610-1821), the Empire of New Mexico (1821-1822), The Republic of Mexico (1823-1846), and the US Territory of

New Mexico (1846+-1912). The Palace of the Governors was and is now the oldest continuously used public building in the United States. Since 1999 it has housed the New Mexico Museum.

Canyon Road is one of the oldest roads still used in the United States. Before it was famous for its half-mile of art galleries in the Historic District of Santa Fe, Canyon Road was a very happening place with bars, saloons, and artist colonies. The Spanish called it "El Camino del cañon" (The road of the canyon). It began as a footpath between the Santa Fe River Valley and Pecos Pueblo trail even before the Spanish arrived. Now it is a long, narrow road that leads to the Sangre de Cristo Mountains, running parallel to the Acequia.

Upper Canyon Road (not a national historic landmark) begins where the historic part of Canyon Road changes from adobe and art galleries to 1600s and 1700s adobe single-family houses. At the base of Upper Canyon is the historic hydroelectric plant that includes a park. Upper Canyon continues to the Randall Davy Audubon Center. A popular outing is to drive to the top of Upper Canyon, and then hike the 3.3-mile Upper Canyon loop. According to Alltrails.com, this is considered a moderately challenging route that takes an average of 1 hour and 46 minutes to complete and is a popular trail for birding, hiking, and running.

Oldest everything

- Oldest capitol in the United States. Santa Fe was settled in 1609

- Oldest Church in the United States. San Miguel Chapel, originally built in 1610

- Oldest House in the United States - De Vargas Street House which rests on part of the foundation of an ancient Indian Pueblo dating around 1200CE

- Santa Fe's oldest hotel: The La Fonda Hotel opened in 1922

- Oldest restaurant in Santa Fe: El Farol originally opened in 1835

- Oldest continuously occupied building in the United States, The Palace of the Governors originally opened in 1610

Historic Hotels of America

The official program of the National Trust
for Historic Preservation

- The La Fonda Hotel
- La Posada de Santa Fe
- Old Santa Fe Inn

National Register of Historic Places (Santa Fe)

- Acequia System of El Rancho de las Golondrinas
- Ricardo Alarid House (534 Alarid St) was built in 1902 and used as the campus of Alvord Elementary Magnet School and Tierra Encantada Charter High School.
- Allison Dormitory (433 Paseo de Peralta) was built in 1930 and is the last surviving building of the Allison Mission School
- Archbishop Lamy's Chapel (Bishop's Lodge Rd)
- Arroyo Hondo Pueblo (address restricted)
- Barrio de Analco Historic District
- Baumann, Jane and Gustave, House and Studio (409 Camino de Las Animas)
- Alfred M. Bergere House (135 Grant Ave.) Built in the 1870s on the Fort Marcy Military Reservation for officer housing.
- Camino Real—La Bajada Mesa Section
- Camino del Monte Sol Historic District (address restricted)
- Connor Hall, (1060 Cerrillos Rd)
- Crespin, Gregorio, House, (132 E. De Vargas St.)
- Davey, Randall, House, (Upper Canyon Rd)
- Delgado Street Bridge

- Digneo-Valdes House, (1231 Paseo de Peralta)

- Dodge-Bailey House, (3775 Old Santa Fe Trail)

- Don Gaspar Bridge

- Don Gaspar Historic District

- El Puente de Los Hidalgos

- El Zaguan, (545 Canyon Rd)

- Fairview Cemetery, (1134 Cerrillos Rd)

- Federal Building, (Cathedral Place at Palace St)

- Fort Marcy Officer's Residence, (116 Lincoln Ave)

- Fort Marcy Ruins, (Off NM 475)

- Hayt-Wientge House, (620 Paseo de la Cuma)

- Hospital, (1060 Cerrillos Rd)

- Jackson, J.B. House, (268 Los Pinos Rd)

- Everret Jones House, (210 Brownell Howland Rd) was designed by architect John Gaw Meem for Bishop and Mrs. Everett Jones

- Kelly, Daniel T. House, (531 East Palace Ave)

- Laboratory of Anthropology, (708 Camino Lejo)

- Las Acequias, (22A Rancho Las Acequias)

- National Park Service Southwest Regional Office, (Old Santa Fe Trail)

- New Mexico Supreme Court Building, (237 Don Gaspar Ave.)

- Palace of the Governors, (Santa Fe Plaza)

- Pueblo of Nambe

- Pueblo of Tesuque

- Reredos of Our Lady of Light, Christo Rey Church, (Canyon Rd)

- San Lazaro (address restricted)

- Santa Fe Historic District

- Santa Fe National Cemetery
- Santa Fe Plaza
- Santa Fe River Park Channel
- School Building Number 2, (1060 Cerrillos Rd)
- Scottish Rite Cathedral, (463 Paseo de Peralta)
- Second Ward School, (312 Sandoval St)
- Seton Village, off US 84
- Shonnard, Eugenie House (address restricted)
- Spiegelberg House (237 East Palace St)
- St. John's College (**1160 Camino De Cruz Blanca**)
- Superintendent's Residence (1060 Cerrillos Rd)
- Tully, Pinckney R House, (136 Grant Ave)
- US Courthouse, (Federal Place)
- Vierra, Carlos House, (1002 Old Pecos Trail)
- Vigil, Donaciano House, (518 Alto St)
- Wheelwright Museum of the American Indian (704 Camino Lejo)

For More Information:

The Historic Santa Fe Foundation (www.historicsantafe.org/)
Historical Society of New Mexico (https://hsnm.org/)

Chapter 6

IT'S
ABOUT
TIME

Significant events and some not so much

SANTA FE TIMELINE

- 1050-1607 Santa Fe was occupied by Pueblo Indian Villages.

- 1492 Isabella and Ferdinand ordered Spain's Jewish community to convert to Catholicism or be expelled causing many to go to Mexico, then be pushed further into New Mexico.

- 1540 Conquistador Don Francisco Vasques de Coronado claimed "Kingdom of New Mexico" for Spain

- 1598 Don Juan de Oñate became the first Governor-General of New Mexico

- 1600s Santa Fe's first paved road (gravel mixture) (Santa Fe New Mexican)

- 1600s+1day Santa Fe's first pothole appeared and is now the oldest in the US

- 1609 – Don Pedro de Peralta appointed second Governor-General of New Mexico and moved the capital to present-day Santa Fe

- 1607-1692 – Spanish soldiers and Franciscan missionaries tried to conquer and convert the Pueblo Indians resulting in a 1680 Indian revolt where most buildings were burned, except for the Palace of the Governors

- 1610 Santa Fe was founded by Governor Pedro de Peralta.

- 1680 Pueblo revolt led to the withdrawal of all Spaniards back to El Paso.

- 1692 Don Diego De Vargas made his first "entrada" into Santa Fe where he accepted the submission of the Pueblos.

- 1692-1821 Santa Fe grew as a prosperous city.

- 1693 Diego de Vargas led a second group of families into New Mexico to re-colonize.

- 1807 Zebulon Pike (of Pike's Peak fame) was arrested by Spanish and taken to Santa Fe

- 1821 Santa Fe Plaza was opened to Americans

- 1821-1846 Santa Fe became the capital of the province of New Mexico, owned by Mexico, which gained independence from Spain.

- 1835 El Farol opens

- 1837 Chimayo Rebellion took place

- 1848 Mexico signed the Treaty of Guadalupe Hidalgo, giving New Mexico and California to the United States.

- 1849 The Santa Fe New Mexican Newspaper was founded as a weekly

- 1851 Construction of St. Francis Cathedral began around the old adobe church

- 1862 The Battle of Glorietta Pass when Union forces beat back the Confederate forces at the Westernmost significant battle of the Civil War stopping the Confederacy's western expansion.

- 1866 Charles Goodnight invented the Chuck Wagon, possibly the first food truck

- 1876 The first Fred Harvey restaurant was opened in Topeka, Kansas

- 1878 Loretto Chapel was completed

- 1880 First rail service to Santa Fe began

- 1880 Jake Gold's Curiosity Shop was opened near Burro Alley (closed 1905)

- 1880 Sunmount Sanitorium was opened to treat tuberculosis

- 1885 Santa Fe School for the Deaf was opened

- 1890 Santa Fe Indian School founded

- 1912 New Mexico became the 47th state

- 1917 The New Mexico Museum of Art was established

- 1918 For the first time, more food was consumed in restaurants than at home

- 1922 The La Fonda Hotel was built

- 1924 The first burning of Zozobra took place

- 1926 Fred Harvey Company purchased the La Fonda Hotel

- 1926 Route 66 opens, bringing opportunities for restaurants all along the route

- 1927 Charles Lindberg landed his plane in Santa Fe

- 1928 Willa Cather's novel, "Death Comes for the Archbishop" was published

- 1928 Santa Fe's first golf course was opened at Bishop's Lodge

- 1928 One of the world's greatest inventions, sliced bread, was actually invented

- 1935 The first art gallery was opened on Canyon Road

- 1937 The paving of Route 66 throughout the state was completed, making Route 66 New Mexico's first fully paved highway

- 1942 The Marine Corps' Navajo Code Talker Program established

- 1943 The Manhattan Project started at the Los Alamos Ranch School for Boys

- 1950 The Concours d'Elegance, also known as the Concours de Santa Fe was first held

- 1956 The Santa Fe Opera was founded

- 1962 The Plaza was named a National Historic Landmark

- 1962 The Institute of American Indian Arts was opened

- 1970's Farolita Canyon Walk began

- 1973 De Vargas Center was opened

- 1974 The Santa Fe Reporter was first published

- 1982 "Foodie" became a thing

- 1984 Santa Fe Institute was founded

- 1988 New York City enacted the first law requiring restaurants with 50 seats or more to provide separate sections for smokers and nonsmokers which soon spread throughout the US.

- 1995 Governor Johnson signed a deal with a dozen Native American tribes allowing casinos and approved the state lottery

- 1998 Five & Dime General Store was opened (Woolworth's was open from 1935-1997 in the same location)

- 2008 Meow Wolf was opened

- 2014 The City of Santa Fe declares March 29 George R.R. Martin Day

- 2015 Violet Crown Theater opened

- 2016: First Lowrider Day on the Plaza occurred

- 2020 On January 20, the Center for Disease Control (CDC) confirmed the first case of COVID-19 in the US in the state of Washington.

- 2020 On March 15, the first restaurants in the US closed because of COVID-19. Ohio Governor Mike DeWine ordered restaurants and bars to close, and within days, other states followed.

- 2020 By March 23, an estimated 7 million restaurant and bar employees are unemployed.

- 2022 For first time, restaurant sales exceeded the pre-pandemic sales of 2019

WHAT'S HAPPENING?

Celebrations and Events in Santa Fe

JANUARY

- **The Souper Bowl** is the Food Depot's signature event and is a soup competition between 25 or more chefs.

- **Three King's Day Celebration** honors New Pueblo Tribal Officials, with most Pueblos open to the public with various dances, including Buffalo, Deer, Eagle, and Elk.

- **St. Ildefonso Feast Day** begins at dawn on January 23rd, when the People of San Ildefonso celebrate with traditional dances, including Deer and Comanche dances.

- **Cars and Coffee** takes place on the first Saturday of each month from 9:00 to 11:00 a.m. on Paseo de Peralta, next to Kakawa Chocolate. Hundreds of cars gather with friendly owners loving to talk cars.

FEBRUARY

- **Santa Fe Restaurant Week** encourages you to sample the food from around 40 restaurants.

- **Santa Fe Jewish Film Festival** introduces films that informs and fosters an understanding of Jewish culture, religion, history, and/or identity. The selections are an eclectic mix of award-winning documentaries, narrative first-run features, and Israeli cinema, representing some of the best films playing the Jewish Film Festival circuit. There are also interviews with the film's producer/director, facilitated discussions, and talks by experts.

- **Art + Sol Santa Fe** allows you to enjoy shows across town, experience world-class culinary offerings, take in exhibitions at galleries and museums, and attend performances highlighting the very best of Santa Fe.

MARCH

- **Santa Fe Home Show & Remodelers Showcase** features the Home Show & Expo, where you can talk with manufacturers, suppliers, retailers, design, and home energy system professionals; the Remodelers Showcase, where you can talk with renovation specialists and see their projects; informative workshops subjects like solar; Kids' Lego Creations Contest. www.SantaFeHomeShow.com

- **ProMusica** Music series throughout March, April, November, and December

APRIL

- **Santa Fe Film Festival** showcases a wide range of films, including feature-length narratives, documentaries, shorts, and experimental works. It embraces diverse voices, genres, and perspectives. Audiences can see everything from thought-provoking dramas to cutting-edge animations. Q&A sessions with directors and actors provide unique insights into the creative process.

- **El Santuario de Chimayo Pilgrimage** occurs on Good Friday; In 2024, it was held on March 29. More than 60,000 pilgrims are estimated to come to Chimayo during Easter week, making this the largest ritual pilgrimage in the United States.

- **ProMusica** concert series throughout April

- **Various tribal dances occur at most Pueblos.** For information, contact Pueblos directly.

MAY

- **Native Treasures Art Market and Auction** takes place Memorial Day weekend at the Santa Fe Community Convention Center. The annual event features over 150 Native artists selected by the Museum of Indian Arts and Culture.

- **Santa Fe International Literary Festival** hosts bestselling and prize-winning authors headline the event, engaging in readings and book signings. There are also in-depth discussions with authors and notable figures who participate in one-on-one conversations, sharing insights and inspirations.

- ♪ **Cloudtop Comedy Festival** features over 50 comedians from across the country, including national headliners, rising stars, and New Mexico's finest locals. It takes place in the Santa Fe Railyard, and tickets are available for single tickets, evening, or weekend wristbands.

- ♪ **SWAIA Native American Fashion Week** features the newest, boldest looks from some of the most exciting Native and Indigenous fashion designers, including runway shows, symposium sessions, and industry parties.

- ♪ **New Mexico Museum of Art Walking Tours** from May through October are led by a docent who highlights the art and architectural history of downtown Santa Fe. Tours leave at 10:00 am from the Museum lobby. Museum admission is included with the purchase of the Art Walking Tour which can be purchased at the front desk on the morning of the tour or online.

JUNE

- ♪ **Currents New Media Festival** is a ten-day affair of artists, experimental video, animation, and documentary artists. This is held at the El Museo Cultural de Santa Fe at 555 Camino de la Familia.

- ♪ **Rodeo de Santa Fe** is one of the top 60 PRCA Rodeos in the nation. Last year's event drew nearly 500 contestants, including many World Champion Cowboys and Cowgirls.

- ♪ **Santa Fe Spring Festival:** From sheep shearing to horno bread baking, you'll see activities and demonstrations showcasing age-old traditions passed down through generations. Children can try crafts tailored just for them, while adults can browse arts and crafts. There will be refreshing hard cider from New Mexico Hard Cider and wine from Sheehan Winery. In 2024, June 1 & 2, 2024, from 10:00 a.m. to 4:00 p.m. El Rancho Golondrinas, 334 Los Pinos Road https://golondrinas.org/events/spring-fest/

JULY

- **Santa Fe Opera** is a world-class opera company that performs in its home venue located just north of Santa Fe. The Santa Fe opera season starts at the end of June and goes through August.

- **Santa Fe Wine Festival** Indulge your senses in a celebration of New Mexico's finest wines, delectable local cuisine, and captivating arts & crafts. Join us for a weekend filled with live music, vibrant dancing, and the unmistakable ambiance of one of the longest-running wine festivals in the state. Savor the flavors of our local wineries as they showcase their best vintages, perfectly complemented by mouthwatering dishes crafted from the freshest regional ingredients. Browse through the eclectic array of arts & crafts, each piece reflecting the unique spirit of our beloved Santa Fe. Come raise a glass with us and toast to three decades of unforgettable moments at the Santa Fe Wine Festival, where every sip is a journey through the heart and soul of New Mexico. Cheers to another 30 years of wine, food, and festivities! In 2024, it will be on July 6 & 7 from 12:00 pm to 6:00 pm. El Rancho Golondrinas, 334 Los Pinos Road https://golondrinas.org/events/santa-fe-wine-festival/

- **Pancakes on the Plaza** is always on the Fourth of July. The Rotary Club cooks pancakes, with local vendors, classic cars, and unique art all around Plaza.

- **The International Folk Art Festival** creates economic opportunities for and with folk artists worldwide who celebrate and preserve folk art traditions. It takes place over three days and showcases 150 artists from 60 different countries, with 11,000 - 20,000 attendees.

- **Fiesta de Los Ninos:** Get your hands on history through tin stamping, rope making, tortilla making, and constructing mini adobe houses. Meet goats, burros, and sheep. See the traditional art of wool spinning, weaving, and dying, and then actually try your hand at these time-honored crafts, guided by skilled artisans. Browse the local arts & crafts. With live entertainment and an array of food trucks, the Santa Fe Fiesta de Los Niños promises an unforgettable experience for children of all ages to discover New Mexico's past. In 2024, July 20 & 21, 2024 between 10:00 am – 4:00 pm El Rancho

Golondrinas, 334 Los Pinos Road. https://golondrinas.org/events/
fiesta-de-los-ninos/

🪶 **Art Santa Fe** is a three-day event, usually in the middle of the month, that takes place at the Santa Fe Community Convention Center for discovering and collecting contemporary and modern art and design.

🪶 **The traditional Spanish Market** attracts as many as 70,000 people and has become the largest juried Spanish Market in the United States. Hundreds of artists and craftsmen show their precious metal jewelry, weaving, ironwork, woodcarving, straw appliqué, pottery, tinwork, colcha, and furniture with traditional New Mexican music and food. Admission is free. In 2024, the dates are July 27 and 28 from 8 a.m. to 5 p.m. Admission is free. This is held on the same days and times as the Contemporary Hispanic Market.

🪶 **Contemporary Hispanic Market** is the world's largest contemporary Hispanic market. All artists are required to be part-Hispanic and full-time residents of New Mexico. The Contemporary Hispanic Market allows artists to show their less traditional work. While the Traditional Spanish Market celebrates age-old techniques and materials, the Contemporary Hispanic Market celebrates the evolution of its art forms, including paintings, jewelry, sculpture, ceramics, textiles, photography, and printmaking. In 2024, the dates are July 27 and 28 from 8 am to 5 pm. Free admission. **This is held on the same days and times as the Traditional Spanish Market.**

AUGUST

🪶 **Santa Fe Beer & Food Festival** at Los Golondrinas where you'll see, taste, and experience the best local breweries, food, live music, games, and artisans. El Rancho de las Golondrinas, 334 Los Pinos Rd.

🪶 **Santa Fe Opera** continues through August.

🪶 **Haciendas: A Parade of Homes** promotes new homes and whole home remodels that present innovative designs and technology to the public. This two-weekend event coincides with the Santa Fe Indian Market.

- **Santa Fe Indian Market** is the largest juried Native American art show in the world attended by an estimated 100,000 people. Over one thousand Native artists from more than one hundred tribal communities in North America and Canada will be here. Artists show their latest work and compete for awards in SWAIA's prestigious judged art competition. Santa Fe's Indian Market has been around for the past 100 years and today generates upwards of 160 million dollars annually in revenues for artists and the community.

- **Fiesta Fine Arts and Crafts Market** is an open-air arts and crafts market featuring booths that line the historic plaza. Select from unique hand-fashioned jewelry, pottery, chic clothing, stylish leather, paintings, photography, wood products, and hand-blown glass. In 2024, it will be held from August 31 to September 2, from 9:00 a.m. to 5:00 p.m.

September

- **Bandstand on the Plaza** features Traditional northern New Mexico music and mariachi music and dancing.

- **Fiesta Desfile de la Gente (Historical/Hysterical Parade)** includes more than 100 floats and vehicles, local marching bands, mariachi, sports teams, queens, floats, and politicians, but expect anything and everything. The parade route is downtown Santa Fe ending at the Plaza. It is one of the events of the Fiesta de Santa Fe.

- **Fiesta Fine Arts and Crafts Market** is an open-air market that features one-of-a-kind treasures from booths that line the historic plaza. Check out unique hand-fashioned jewelry, pottery, chic clothing, stylish leather, paintings, photography, wood products, and hand-blown glass. Meet the artists and discuss their work.

- **Burning of Zozobra** This event is a really big deal here. In 2023, over 71,000 attended this event which is held at Fort Marcy Park. With so many people attending this event, security is strict, so bring as little as possible. Everyone will be searched with a wand. Bring only clear bags as every other type of bag is not allowed, including purses. No coolers, no pets, no strollers, no backpacks, and no folding chairs. Zozobra takes place on the Friday before Labor Day, opening at 4:00

pm with live entertainment and concluding with the main event, the burning of Zozobra, starting around 8:30 pm.

- **Desfile de Los Niños (Pet Parade)** takes place on Santa Fe Plaza between 9:00 a.m. and 10:45 a.m. In 2024, it took place on September 7.

- **Fiesta de Santa Fe** is three days of celebration that includes a reenactment of Don Diego de Vargas's return to the city, a children's pet parade, the Historical/Hysterical Parade, the Fiesta Ball, and Roman Catholic masses. During the festival, the Santa Fe Plaza has arts & crafts and food booths, and mariachis play throughout the city. Fiestas concludes with mass at the St. Francis Cathedral followed by a candlelight procession to the Cross of the Martyrs.

- **Santa Fe Renaissance Faire** happens around the middle of the month. Meet the Royal Court of the Kingdom of Golondrinas and witness real combat at the tournament. Immerse in the sights and sounds of the Middle Ages with live medieval music, dancing, a costume contest, medieval arts and crafts, and sample the finest libations from New Mexico's own Hard Cider, Beer Creek Brewing, and Sheehan Winery.

- **Santa Fe Open Studio Tour** allows a peek into the studios of about a hundred artists in Santa Fe.

- **Santa Fe Wine and Chile Fiesta** has become an annual five-day event celebrating the best Santa Fe has to offer with over 60 participating restaurants and 90 winery partners. Over 3,500 guests arrive in Santa Fe each September for this one-of-a-kind Fiesta. https://santafewineandchile.org/

October

- **Santa Fe International Film Festival (SFiFF)** was founded in 2009, it is now one of the top annual events and the largest event of its kind in New Mexico, with more than 300 hours of programming each season. In 2023, over 133,700 attendees saw major Academy Award winners, top international films, and undiscovered indie gems. SFiFF was recognized nationally by IndieWire Magazine as "a young Sundance" and was named one of Moviemaker Magazine's "Coolest Film Festivals on the Planet" and "50 Festivals Worth the Entry Fee."

- **Albuquerque International Balloon Fiesta** is a nine-day event, making it the largest ballooning event and the most photographed event in the world. It's pretty spectacular. The Balloon Fiesta Park's launch field is 54 football fields, necessary to accommodate the 500+ balloons that launch during this event.

- **Santa Fe Harvest Festival** Learn how to make red chile ristras, pick the perfect pumpkin, stomp grapes by foot, and discover the art of making corn husks with hands-on demonstrations. Browse local arts & crafts with period-correct dressed docents guiding your journey through the past. Try Golondrinas Gold Ale, brewed from Golondrinas Hops by Beer Creek Brewing or Sheehan Winery's finest New Mexican wines. Try a hayride around the ranch. In 2024, October 5 & 6, 2024, between 10:00 am to 4:00 pm. El Rancho Golondrinas, 334 Los Pinos Road

- **Spirits of New Mexico** is where New Mexico's past spirits come to life. Gather around campfires and lantern-lit paths as you listen to tales of ghosts who once roamed. This transforms into a family-friendly yet spooky Halloween atmosphere. Enjoy live entertainment and sip beer and hard cider from New Mexico Hard Cider and local cuisine. This is the only nighttime event to celebrate the Spirits of New Mexico. In 2024, October 26, 2024, between 5:00 pm – 9:00 pm. El Rancho Golondrinas, 334 Los Pinos Road

November

- **Holiday Tree Lighting on the Plaza** typically takes place on a Friday during the last week of November. Santa and Mrs. Claus arrive by vintage fire truck at 5:15 p.m., and at 6:15 p.m., the Plaza lights are switched on to officially kick off the holiday season! After the lights are lit, there's music, hot cocoa, cookies, and more, continuing until 8 p.m., with decorations up for the remainder of the holidays.

- **SWAIA Winter Indian Market** features over 150 vendors displaying traditional and contemporary artworks; enjoy musical and dance performances; participate in an in-person silent auction and raffles;

and a variety of delicious food offerings.

♪ **ProMusica** concert series throughout November

♪ **Lensic Performing Arts Center** always has great events this month

December

♪ **Santa Fe Farolito Walk on Canyon Road** occurs on Christmas Eve. Thousands stroll (never walk) on Canyon Road passing by small bonfires, hearing street musicians playing and singers singing traditional holiday songs. You'll see the occasional hot chocolate, biscochitos, and luminarias along the road, too. Many of the galleries are open so make sure you stop in and be sure to dress warmly. The event begins at sundown. Don't even think about bringing your car, there's no place to park, plus many of the streets in the area are closed to cars.

♪ **New Year's Eve on the Plaza** begins at 8 pm with the Plaza warmed by stationary heaters and cozy piñon bonfires. Hear live music from Santa Fe's favorite bands while The Kiwanis Club of Santa Fe provides free hot chocolate and biscochitos, New Mexico's official state cookie. Around 11:45 pm, the mayor and city officials invite the crowd to count down to the new year. Because Santa Fe is "the City Different", nothing will drop. When the countdown ends, a colorful Zia symbol hand-crafted by a traditional local artisan will rise at the stroke of midnight with fireworks launched from Santa Fe's most historic hotel, La Fonda on the Plaza.

♪ **ProMusica** concert series throughout December

Chapter 7

ART AND ARCHITECTURE

WHY IS ART SO BIG IN SANTA FE?

Several factors developed over time into a perfect storm for Santa Fe to stand out in art. It all started with Native American pottery, weaving, and architecture. Then, much later in the sixteenth century, Spanish colonists brought their style of art with wood carving, embroidery, tinwork, furniture, and painting. Then, in the early 20th century, East Coast artists discovered Santa Fe's unique colors, shapes, and lights and introduced them to Santa Fe's hospitality, charm, and simplicity of lifestyle.

But there were other factors in play, too.

- Santa Fe's Sunmount Sanitorium was a major influence in helping people rehabilitate from tuberculosis. After being cured by the health benefits of Santa Fe's dry, desert climate, many stayed.

- Santa Fe's high-desert landscape, colorful sunsets, 300-plus days of blue skies, and colonial architecture were major attractions for artists.

- Santa Fe preserved its ties to Spanish, Native American, and Mexican traditions over its 400-year history as New Mexico's state capital.

- Santa Fe is a shopping destination for art in general and artisan goods in particular. From textiles and pottery to jewelry, the city offers an incredible assortment of handcrafted items.

- Santa Fe's local and indigenous art scene attracts both artists and collectors.

- Santa Fe's many festivals and events celebrate and support folk artists from all over the world, creating economic opportunities and promoting art traditions.

As a result of the above, Santa Fe has over 300 galleries, which, according to Forbes, makes it the third-largest art market in the United States, just behind New York and Los Angeles. Not bad for a city with a population of 90,000.

Four Art Districts

Downtown: Art, history, and restaurants are everywhere around the Plaza. Under the Palace of the Governors portal, you'll find Native American arts and crafts, plus, very near, the Georgia O'Keeffe Museum and the New Mexico Museum of Art.

Canyon Road: About 100 art galleries, from traditional to contemporary, line both sides of Canyon Road. There are many gallery openings on Fridays. On Christmas Eve, don't miss the Farolito walk on Canyon. On Christmas Eve, Canyon Road is shut down for cars, and pedestrians are only allowed. Most galleries are open, carolers sing, and at least for one night, all is well as thousands walk Canyon.

Railyard: The Railyard has many modern and contemporary art galleries, along with the Farmer's Market on Saturdays and the Railyard Artisan Market on Sundays. While here, visit the Vladem Museum, SITE Santa Fe, and its many restaurants and bars.

SFXL: According to the Santa Fe Gallery Association, this is Santa Fe's newest and largest art district, first launched when Meow Wolf opened in 2016. Since then, this area has seen rapid growth as artists reinvent a part of town previously known for its bowling alley and car repair shops but now has galleries, digital arts, food trucks, and rehearsal studios. It covers Museum Hill on the East side, down to the old Outlet Mall on the South, Second Street Studios, Baca and Lena Streets on the North, and Rufina in the West.

ART, ART, and MORE ART

Santa Fe Artists Market: Local artists display their art, jewelry, and other crafts on Saturdays at the Railyard, West Casitas, just north of the Water Tower. A really fun place to explore. Hours: 9:00 am to 2:00 pm March through December

Santa Fe Open Studios: Over a hundred artists open their studios in September.

Canyon Road Galleries: 100 galleries line a half mile of Canyon Road.

The International Folk Art Market (IFAM) showcases folk art from more than 50 different countries in July.

Santa Fe Art Week: During Santa Fe Art Week, 100+ events are planned across the city's museums, attractions, and galleries during the last week in July.

Contemporary Hispanic Market: The world's largest contemporary Hispanic market happens every July in the Plaza. You'll find paintings, printmaking, sculpture, photography, furniture, jewelry, ceramics, weaving, and more. Entry is free. It runs from 8:00 a.m. to 5:00 p.m. for two days.

Traditional Spanish Market: The Spanish Market is the oldest and largest juried art show of its kind in the nation. Juried artists from New Mexico and Colorado show their work in 19 traditional categories. The market includes dance, music, food, and all things traditional in New Mexico, attracting tens of thousands of visitors each year. It has approximately 200 adult and mentored youth artists. Entry is free and runs from 8:00 a.m. to 5:00 p.m. There is also a Winter Spanish Market in early December.

Santa Fe Indian Market: The Santa Fe Indian Market is the largest juried Native American art show in the world. Each August, an estimated 100,000 people attend. It began in 1922 and is put on by The Southwestern Association for Indian Arts. It sponsors over 1,000 Native artists from more than 100 tribal communities in North America and Canada.

Meow Wolf: Meow Wolf is a hip venue for contemporary interactive art exhibits and music. In 2015, George R. R. Martin pledged 2.7 million dollars for a long-term lease and renovation of a vacant bowling alley in Santa Fe for the collective to develop a permanent interactive art installation. It also hosts local and regional indie music performances. By 2022, the company had grown to 980 employees, with a revenue of $158 million. The founders were Matt King, Emily Montoya, Caity Kennedy, Benji Geary, Corvas Brinkerhoff, Sean Di Ianni, and Vince Kadlubek.

Capitol Art Collection at the Roundhouse

Starting in 1991, the Roundhouse has hosted a permanent installation of over 600 pieces of art from over 600 New Mexican artists collected by the state. This is one of the best-kept secrets in Santa Fe. Pass it on.

Georgia O'Keeffe Museum

The O'Keeffe Museum is home to over 3,000 works, with 1,149 pieces created by Georgia O'Keeffe. The museum also presents special exhibitions and has shown works by more than 140 other artists.

New Mexico Museum of Art

(New Mexico Museum of Art-Vladem Contemporary and the Plaza Building)

- The New Mexico Museum of Art is the oldest art museum in the state. Built in 1917, the building itself is a work of art, considered a masterpiece of Pueblo Revival architecture. It is one of four state museums that are part of the Museum of New Mexico system. The museum's mission is to collect, preserve, exhibit, and interpret the art of New Mexico and the greater Southwest. 107 West Palace Avenue

- The Vladem Contemporary is a spectacular building with an open floor plan, high ceilings, and controlled lighting that mirrors the flexible, stripped-down gallery style of today. It is in the Railyard at 404 Montezuma Avenue.

Museum of Spanish Colonial Art

The Museum of Spanish Colonial Art, with 3,700 objects in various collections, represents the most comprehensive compilation of Spanish Colonial art of its kind. Among the various media featured are Santos (painted and sculpted images of saints), textiles, tinwork, silverwork, goldwork, ironwork, straw appliqué, ceramics, furniture, and books.

Museum of International Folk Art

Opened in 1953, the Museum of International Folk Art is home to the world's largest collection of folk art, with more than 135,000 artifacts.

Wheelwright Museum of the American Indian

The Wheelwright Museum of the American Indian offers exhibitions of contemporary and historic Native American art, including little-known genres and solo shows by living Native American artists.

Museum of Indian Arts & Culture

The Museum of Indian Arts & Culture has an extensive collection of Native art and cultural materials that tell the stories of the people of the Southwest from pre-history through contemporary times.

New Mexico History Museum

The New Mexico History Museum has numerous interactive exhibits illustrating the history of Native peoples, Spanish colonialists, New Mexico's Mexican Period, and travel along the Santa Fe Trail. This museum includes the Palace of the Governors, the Palace Press, and the Fray Angelico Chavez History Library and Photo Archives. www.nmhistorymuseum.org

SITE Santa Fe

SITE Santa Fe presents three to four exhibitions, dozens of unique public programs, and a range of programs for young people each year. It presents artists from around the world while also supporting locally based artists with career development opportunities and significant exhibition opportunities. Admission is free. It is closed on Tuesday and Wednesday. 1606 Paseo de Peralta. (https://sitesantafe.org/)

Art Vault

The Art Vault is the Carl & Marilynn Thoma Foundation's newest exhibition space. Located in the Railyard Arts District, the 3,500-square-foot gallery is the only digital art collection open to the public in the Southwest.

Santa Fe Arts Commission: "Art in Public Places"

The Art in Public Places Program began in 1985, and it includes more than 80 artworks in many media, styles, and themes. Public art can be found in civic buildings, along the Santa Fe Trails transit system, and in public parks.

Artist selections are held for each public art project by a community selection committee appointed by the Arts and Culture Department Staff. The committee reviews artist qualifications and proposals. Their recommendations are then forwarded to the Arts Commission for recommendation to the Governing Body for approval. Upon approval, the artist enters into a professional services contract with the city to design, fabricate, and install the selected artwork. The Arts and Culture Department implements the Art in Public Places program.

Below is a list of the permanent portfolio:

Santa Fe Municipal Airport
"Untitled Tri-Culture Sculpture", Jerry West and Charles Southard
Santa Fe Convention Center
"A Mano" by Jane Chavez

"Airstream" by Kristin Lora

"Cedar in Rocks" by Leslie McNamara

"Energy Field & Water" by Nancy Reyner

"Family" by Roxanne Swentzell

"Furniture Grouping" by David Burlingand Dennis Esquivel
   "Furniture Grouping" by Jason Mossman and Richard Gonzales and Robin Speas

"Gibraltar Rock" by Flo Perkins

"Old Time Spring Time" by Sam Leyba

"Santa Fe Current" by Colette Hosmer

"Santa Fe de la Vega, Spain and Santa Fe, New Mexico" by Frederico Vigil

"Seripente de Cascable" by Jane Chavez

"Sopero Set" by Camilla Trujillo

"The Tourist" by Gail Gash Taylor

"Thunder Whorl" by Ed Archie NoiseCat

"Transition" by Sandra Duran Wilson

"Untitled, Three Panel Fabric Quilt", by Margaret Favour

"What Lies Beneath" by Joan Zalenski

Herb Martinez Park
   "UP", Steel by TC Hicks

South Side Branch Library
   "Arroyo Chamiso" by Stuart Keeler and Michael Machic"
   "Children's Fountain" by Linda Strong
   "Reference Point" by Amy Chaloupka
   "Untitled Tinwork Panels" by Jimmy Romero
   "View from Below" by Stuart Keeler and Michael Machic
   "Waterworks" by Don Kennel
   "Woven Olla" by Randy Walker

La Familia Medical Center
   "Mother and Child" by Tim Klabunde
   "Revedios" by Glen Strock

City Hall
   San Francisco de Assisi, by Andrea Bacigalupa
   Recuerdos y Suenos de Santa Fe by Jerry West

Santa Fe River Park
"Seven Archangels" by Jose Lucero
"Untitled Tree Carving" by Don Kennell

Acequia Madre School
"Acequia Madre" by Frederico Vigil

Adam Gabriel Armijo Park
"St. Francis" by Ben and Pete Ortega

Airport Road
"Untitled Bus Shelter", by Joe Tyler

Amelia White Park
"The Korean War Memorial" by Kim Crowley

Botulph Road
"Waveform Railing"

Burro Alley
"Homage to the Burro" by Charles Southard

Camino Lejo
"Journey's End" by Reynaldo
"Sonny" Rivera and Richard Borkovetz

De Vargas Park
"Trail of Dreams, Trail of Ghost" by Catherine Widgery

Frenchy's Field
"Trail of Dreams, Trail of Ghost" by Catherine Widgery

Genoveva Chavez Community Center
"Live Moves" by Walter kravitz

Hillside Park
"El Diferente" by Mac Vaughn

La Farge Library
"New Mexico Quilt" by Janet Maher with Marie Steward

Las Acequias Park
"La Acequia" by Hank Saxe and Cynthia Patterson

Magistrate Court
"Judicial History of Santa Fe" by Zara Kriegstein

Monica Roybal Center
"Suenos de Juventud" by Sam Leyba

Paseo de Peralta and Grant Avenue
"The Founding of Santa Fe" by Dave McGarity

Ragle Park
"400th Anniversary Commemoration Project" Dolmitic Limestone by Madeline Wiener

Barrio la Canada Neighborhood Gateway by Paula Castillo

St. Francis/Zia Pedestrian Underpass by Bobbe Besold

Sandoval Parking Garage
"Mesa", by Rudolf Hunziker

Santa Fe Railyard Park
"Railyard Bus Shelter" by Helmut Hillenkamp and Christry Hengst

Santa Fe Trails Transit
"Hands" by Bobbe Besold

South Cerrillos Road
"Cuento del Camino /Road Stores" by Mary Antonia Wood and Christopher Gibson

Torreon Park
"El Torreon de El Torreon" by Pedro Romero

Veteran's Memorial Highway
"Untitled, Pedestrian Underpass" by Frederico Vigil

Water Street
"Fountainhead Rock" by Tomas Lipps and George Gonzales

Franklin Miles Park
"St. Francis" by Ivan Dimitrov

Alto Park
"Our Lady of Guadalupe" by Gabriel Vigil

Camino Alire
"Camino Alire Bridge" by Susan Wink

Architecture

The more research I did on Santa Fe's architecture, the more muddied (or stuccoed) it got. With just a little exaggeration, Santa Fe seems to have between 3 and 420 architectural styles, depending on who you ask or where you look. But here is my best shot at it.

Pueblo Architecture (pre-1600s) Before European colonization, the indigenous Pueblo people inhabited the region. Their architectural style featured adobe structures with thick walls, flat roofs, and earthy tones, blending with the natural landscape. The more traditional pueblo houses were very simple and were built using large adobe bricks (made from clay and water) to ensure the home remained cool and comfortable. The Pueblo style is rooted in ancient history and draws inspiration from early Native American dwellings. Key features include round walls and corner fireplaces, 'vigas' (round, exposed roof beams), flat roofs, and 'portales' (covered porches).

Spanish Colonial (1600s-1800s): With the arrival of Spanish settlers in the 17th century, Santa Fe saw the introduction of Spanish Colonial architecture. This style often included adobe construction, flat roofs, thick walls, and courtyards. Churches and government buildings were prominent examples of this style, which was characterized by simplicity and functionality.

Territorial (Mid-19th Century to Early 20th Century) developed after the American annexation in 1846, when New Mexico became a territory of the United States and continued until its statehood in 1912. It combined elements of Spanish Colonial architecture with Victorian influences. Features included pitched metal roofs, ornate wooden trim, and decorative elements. This style marked a departure from traditional adobe construction for some buildings. The basis was the Greek Revival style, which was popular during this period. Hand-made windows were replaced with mill-made double-sashed and small-paned windows, which were often capped with triangular pediments. Slender, rectangular columns replace the rounded, heavier supports of the Pueblo-style portals. The woodwork was painted white. Kilned brick produced locally was used as a coping to protect the exposed adobe parapets. In the 1870s, adobe brick began to be plastered with lime to prevent erosion since exposed adobe was prone to wear from rain and snow, but later, cement stuccoing was used.

Pueblo Revival (Early to Mid-20th Century). In the early 20th century, there was a renewed interest in Pueblo architecture. The Pueblo Revival style emerged, drawing inspiration from the traditional adobe structure of the indigenous Pueblo People. Characteristics included flat roofs, rounded edges, exposed wooden beams (vigas), and earth tones. Prominent architects like John Gaw Meen helped popularize this style. Key distinguishing features included exterior stucco (meant to imitate the adobe walls of the Indian pueblo) and projecting roof rafters called "Vigas," which are generally round or square and protrude from the wall near the roofline but are decorative. Projecting round scuppers/ roof drains, called "canales" can also be found or substituted for vigas. The roof of the Pueblo Revival structure is usually flat. Better examples of the style have rounded corners and battered exterior walls. Straight-headed, multi-light windows are often recessed deep within the façade. Large, heavy doors, many with arched tops, are also common. Sheltered courtyards and patios, enclosed by low walls, often utilize built-in benches, called "bancos," which protrude from walls. Also found on the inside or outside were small carved "nichos" or niches in the walls, which were designed for storing decorations or religious objects. **Main visual element:** Soft, rounded corners and exposed wooden support beams.

Territorial Revival (Early to Mid-20th Century) At the same time as the Pueblo Revival movement, the Territorial style was revived. This style incorporated Spanish Colonial and Territorial architecture elements, often featuring pitched roofs with wooden vigas, stucco exteriors, and decorative details reminiscent of the Territorial period. For example, weather-resistant fired brick coping is applied to parapet tops to preserve the erodible mud-finished walls below for longer periods. Courses of brickwork are often laid in a Neoclassical dental pattern. Square-cut posts and headers support entry portals without corbels. Roof beams are cut back to the same front plane as the headers rather than projecting beyond the header surface. Plaster or wooden fascia boards are applied to hide roof beam ends, resulting in weather protection and simplification of visual impact. Dimensional lumber is used for decorative balustrades, shutters, and window or door surrounds that often have a Neoclassical triangular pediment. **Main visual element:** Flat roofs and hard, angular edges, often capped with brick around the roofline.

Contemporary (Mid-20th Century to Present)

In more recent years, Santa Fe has seen a blend of architectural styles, including modern and contemporary designs, alongside continued reverence for traditional adobe and Pueblo Revival architecture. While newer buildings may incorporate modern materials and construction techniques, there is often a nod to the region's cultural and architectural heritage.

In the early 21st century, modern construction materials were sometimes used in conjunction with adobe to ensure stronger and more durable structures. Modern architects now infuse historic styles with contemporary designs. Sleek lines, sustainable materials, and innovative layouts create a fresh look for Santa Fe in the 21st century.

Note 1: The old Santa Fe vernacular manner of architecture (see note 3) is partially to blame for why New Mexico had such a difficult time in gaining statehood. Federal officials found Santa Fe's long and low mud huts to be un-American. So, Santa Fe tried to look more "American" by imitating architectural styles from the East Coast. But after New Mexico gained statehood, this was a problem. Santa Fe was becoming bland and homogenized, turning Santa Fe's unique look into "Anywhere USA." As you might suspect, this caused a movement away from the 'Americanization Period' to the "Santa Fe Style," preserving old Santa Fe's qualities, attracting tourism, and population growth.

Note 2: The New Mexico Style (pueblo and territorial revival styles) is one of the few architectural styles intentionally developed to attract tourists. Originating in Santa Fe at the turn of the 20th century, the style spread across the Southwest.

Note 3: Vernacular architecture refers to the style of buildings and structures that are designed and constructed based on local traditions, materials, and techniques rather than by professional architects. It represents the everyday architecture of a particular region or community, shaped by factors such as climate, culture, available resources, and local needs.

For more information,
Visit the Historic Santa Fe Foundation
www.historicsantafe.org/

Chapter 8

LITERARY
SANTA FE

The Santa Fe International Literary Festival is held in mid-May at the Santa Fe Community Convention Center. It brings together around 20 world-renowned authors and passionate readers. Remarkably, this festival has become a significant event in Santa Fe in such a short time since it only began in 2022.

We are incredibly proud of the Pulitzer Prize winners
who have chosen to live in Santa Fe

Pulitzer Prize Winners and Nominees

- **Cather, Willa** (1873-1947) won the Pulitzer Prize for *One of Ours* and wrote about the life of Archbishop Lamy in *Death Comes for the Archbishop*. She stayed in Santa Fe in the 1920s.

- **DeBuys, William** (born 1949) was a teacher at the College of Santa Fe. His works include *Mountain Range* and *A Village Life,* which was a finalist for the Pulitzer Prize. He lived in Santa Fe in the 2000s when he taught Documentary Studies at the College of Santa Fe. He was a founder of the Santa Fe Conservation Trust.

- **Fraser, Caroline** obtained her Ph.D. from Harvard University, and she is the author of several works, including *God's Perfect Child: Living and Dying in the Christian Science Church* and the Pulitzer Prize-winning biography *Prairie Fires: The American Dreams of Laura Ingalls Wilder*. She lives in Santa Fe.

- **La Farge, Oliver** (1901-1963) was an anthropologist and an ethnologist who wrote many fictional works about New Mexico including *Laughing Boy*, a novel that won the Pulitzer Prize in 1930, *Enemy Gods,* and his autobiography, *Raw Materials*. He was president of the Association on American Indian Affairs and wrote a column for the New Mexican. He was a long-time resident of Santa Fe.

- **Bill Mauldin** (1921-2003) was an editorial cartoonist best known for his "Willie and Joe" cartoons about the average soldier in World War II. He won two Pulitzer Prizes for Editorial Cartooning in 1945 and 1959. He is also the author and illustrator of numerous books, including *A Sort of a Saga*. He lived in Santa Fe from 1970 to 1997.

- **McCarthy, Cormac** (1933-2023) has won many awards, including the Pulitzer Prize for *The Road* and the National Book Award for *All the Pretty Horses*. The film adaptation of his book *No Country for Old Men* won four Academy Awards including Best Picture. He was a Fellow at the Santa Fe Institute.

- **Momaday, N. Scott** (1934-2024) was an author, poet, and painter. He earned a bachelor's degree in political science at UNM and a master's and Ph.D. from Stanford. He received the Pulitzer Prize for *House Made of Dawn* in 1968. He was the artist for the poster for the 1990 Santa Fe Indian Market. He received the Governor's Art Award in 1996 and the National Medal of Arts in 2007.

- **Niemeyer, Lucian** (1937-2016) was a photographer and author of several books, including *Desert Wetlands and New Mexico: Images of a Land and Its People* and *The People: Pueblo Portraits and Africa, The Holocausts of Rwanda and Sudan*, which was nominated for a Pulitzer Prize. He lived in Santa Fe.

- **Oliphant, Pat** (born 1935) is a political cartoonist who lives in Santa Fe.

- **Shepard, Sam** (1943-2017) was a playwright and actor. Scholar with the Santa Fe Institute. Pulitzer Prize for Drama in 1979 for the play *Buried Child*. Author of *Sam Shepard New Mexico*. He lived in Santa Fe from the 1980s.

- **Sze, Arthur** (born 1950) is a poet, translator, writer, professor, and professor emeritus at the Institute of American Indian Arts. He has won a National Book Award for Poetry and is the author of many poetry collections, including *The Ginkgo Light* and *Compass Rose*, a finalist for the 2015 Pulitzer Prize for Poetry. He was the first Poet Laureate of Santa Fe, serving from 2006 to 2008.

The Joy of Independent Bookstores in Santa Fe

- **Allá** carries one of the largest selections of new and out-of-print books in Spanish, including children's books. It also carries English-language books about Latin America and the U.S. Southwest. It is open noon—6:00 pm Monday through Saturday, and it is closed Sunday. The address is 102 W San Francisco St, suite 20.

- **The Ark** is a metaphysical bookstore that also carries gift cards, candles, crystals, incense, and jewelry. Open Monday-Saturday 10:00 am to 6:00

pm, closed Sunday. 133 Romero St

- **Beastly Books** is owned by George R.R. Martin. Its emphasis is on mainly science fiction and fantasy books; but it hosts many free events, has autographed and collectible books, and has coffee! Open 12:00 pm to 7:00 pm Wednesday & Thursday, 11:00 am to 7:00 pm Friday & Saturday, noon to 4:00 pm Sunday. Closed Monday & Tuesday. 418 Montezuma Ave.

- **Bee Hive** is a children's bookstore that also hosts kids writing workshops. Open daily from 10:30 am to 4:00 pm, closed Sundays. 328 Montezuma Ave

- **Big Star Books and Music** buys, sells, and trades used books and CDs. Open Tuesday to Saturday, 10:00 am to 7:00 pm, Sunday, 12:00 pm to 7:00 pm 329 Garfield St

- **Book Mountain Paperback Exchange** is the only paperback book exchange in Santa Fe. Open 11:00 am to 7:00 pm Tuesday to Friday; 10:00 am to 9:00 pm Saturday. 1302 Osage Ave

- **Books of Interest**: Carries fine-used books on art, photography, art technique, the Southwest, New Mexico, Native American art and culture, poetry, literature, Eastern and Western philosophy and religion, history, nature, science, gardening, and cooking. It also carries used CDs and vinyl. Open Monday – Saturday, 11:00 am to 5:00 pm. 1333 Cerrillos Rd

- **Collected Works Bookstore** is Santa Fe's oldest, independent, woman-owned bookstore. It is a great place to browse and get a cup of coffee. It is well known for its 70 author/poet events each year. The bookstore is open from 9:00 a.m. to 5:00 p.m. daily, and the coffee shop is open from 9:00 a.m. to 4:00 p.m. daily. 202 Galisteo St.

- **Dumont Maps & Books of the West** is an Antiquarian bookstore specializing in Western Americana, including antique maps, out-of-print and rare books, rare and unusual ephemera, and antique prints. Open Tuesday to Saturday, 11:00 am to 5:00 pm. 407 West San Francisco St.

- **Garcia Street Books** is a great local bookstore. It is open daily from 10:00 a.m. to 5:00 p.m. and is located at 376 Garcia St, right next to Downtown Subscription Coffee Shop.

- **Good Stuff—Café Vinyl** has just about everything: coffee, vinyl records, lots of books, T-shirts, and sunglasses. It is open daily from 11:00 a.m. to 6:00 p.m. 401 W. San Francisco St.

- **Op.cit Books.** If you close your eyes and picture an independent bookstore, Op. Cit is what you'll see: stacks of books in seeming chaos. But do not fear. Incredibly, they know where everything is. The bookstore is in the DeVargas Mall and is open 8:00 a.m. to 7:00 p.m. Monday through Saturday and 8:00 a.m. to 6:00 p.m. Sunday.

- **Photo-Eye Bookstore** Large collection of Surprise! photo books. But wait! There's more. It also has a gallery and holds auctions. Open 10:00 am to 5:30 pm, Tuesday to Saturday. 1300 Rufina Circle, Suite A3

- **Purple Fern Bookstore** is open 10:00 am to 6:00 pm Monday to Friday, 10:00 to 5:00 pm Saturday, and closed Sunday. Located in El Dorado at 7 Ave Vista Grande # D5

- **St. John's College Bookstore** carries an eclectic collection of books, with academics mixed in with fun and intellectual content. It is open Monday through Friday from 10:00 a.m. to 5:00 p.m. at 1160 Camino De Cruz Blanca.

- **Travel Bug Specialty Book Store** is all about travel. Big sections on Santa Fe and New Mexico plus every state and every country. There are also books on hiking, visiting, and living with seemingly thousands of maps worldwide, including travel accessories and a coffee bar. When you get completely travel-weary, it even has a limited taproom. Check for author readings, language lessons, and more. Open Monday to Saturday, 9:00 am to 6:00 pm, and Sunday, noon to 4:00 pm. 839 Paseo De Peralta

Poets Laureate of Santa Fe

The City of Santa Fe Arts and Culture Department's Poet Laureate program honors a Santa Fe poet and recognizes poetry's place in our community's cultural tradition and civic life. The Poet Laureate is an ambassador of the art form, literature, literacy, and storytelling and works to inspire the next generation of poets and their readers.

Requirements/Qualifications:
- The poet must be a Santa Fe City or County resident for at least two years or have been employed in Santa Fe County for at least two

years and continue to live and/or work in the city throughout the appointment.

◈ The poet must have a significant publication history in a variety of journals and media, and preferably at least one book in print or under contract from a reputable press (excluding self-published and vanity presses); have recognition in the field; and demonstrate literary excellence

◈ The poet must have demonstrated a previous commitment to promoting awareness of poetry

◈ The poet must be 21 years of age and older

1st Poet Laureate   Arthur Sze 2005-2008
Valerie Martinez 2008 – 2010
Joan Logghe 2010 – 2012
Jon Davis 2012 – 2014
Elizabeth Jacobson 2019 – 2021
Darryl Wellington 2021 – 2023
Tommy Archuleta 2024-2026

INTELLECTUAL
SANTA FE

𝒿 **Global Santa Fe** is an education-based nonprofit organization that stimulates dialogue around critical world issues. Global Santa Fe's mission is to elevate global awareness, promote citizen diplomacy, and offer opportunities for the next generation of global citizens. Various programs and events encourage dialogue, cultural exchange, and student engagement. Global Santa Fe provides world-class speakers covering global issues, including politics, culture, and international relations, that expose diverse points of view. In partnership primarily with the U.S. Department of State, international leaders come to New Mexico every year, creating authentic connections. Through exposing students to critical global issues, students in Santa Fe and New Mexico will expand their horizons.

𝒿 **The Indian Arts Research Center (IARC)** bridges creativity and scholarship by supporting initiatives and projects in Native American studies, art history, and creative expression. It illuminates the intersections of the social sciences, humanities, and arts by providing fellowship opportunities for artists to engage in uninterrupted creativity; fostering dialogue among artists, researchers, scholars, and community members through seminars and symposia; nurturing future arts and museum professionals through experiential training; and promoting study and exploration of the IARC collection of Native American arts. The IARC Collection is considered to be one of the most remarkable collections of Southwestern Native American art in the world. Representing a broad range of works, this valuable collection's foundation initially was formed in 1922 and has since grown to over 12,000 items.

𝒿 **The National Center for Genome Resources** (NCGR) was founded in 1994 as an independent non-profit, with the mission of providing software and database support for the Department of Energy's Human Genome Project at Los Alamos National Laboratory. It is a not-for-profit research institute that innovates, collaborates, and educates in genomic data science. NCGR partners with government, industry, and academia to drive biological discovery and delivers value through expertise in experimental design, software, computation, data integration, and training a skilled workforce. NCGR has been at the forefront of studying DNA with computers. NCGR occupies a purpose built 32,000 square foot facility completed in 2000. The focus of NCGR's research has changed

149

over the years but its overall goals have remained consistent, which is to do independent research and to provide community software support for the study of genes and genomes, including genomic medicine and agricultural science. From 2008-2018 NCGR operated the New Mexico Genome Center. In 2018, in response to changing forces in the sequencing market, NCGR chose to focus exclusively on data analytics.

NCGR has demonstrated a track record of successful software, bioinformatics, and research collaborations and an impressive record of publications in high-impact journals. NCGR has an ongoing scientific impact in Genomic Data Science related to agricultural and forestry organisms, model systems, human biology, ecologically important organisms, and the rapidly developing field of the microbiome.

⤷ **Santa Fe Community College** offers more than 100 degrees and certificate programs, enrolling over 4,000 students in for-credit courses leading to an associate degree and 5,000 students in contract or continuing education. The student-faculty ratio is 12-to-1. It offers over 150 continuing education classes to the community. The school has an open admissions policy and offers credit for life experiences. SFCC is designated a Best for Vets and Military Friendly school.

⤷ **Santa Fe Institute:** The Santa Fe Institute is a private, not-for-profit, independent research and education center that works to bring strong quantitative methods and a range of interdisciplinary perspectives to bear on significant questions for science and society. It was founded in 1984, the institute where scientists deal with the most significant complex phenomena. Inter-disciplinary research is undertaken in a collaborative manner, with scientists coming to the Santa Fe Institute from various universities, research institutes, and government agencies. The institute came into existence through the continuous collaboration and knowledge sharing between George Cowan (a senior fellow at Los Alamos Laboratory) and other colleagues at the laboratory. The founding members were George Cowan, David Pines, Stirling Colgate, Murray Gell-Mann, Nick Metropolis, Herb Anderson, Peter A. Carruthers, and Richard Slansky. Only Pines and Gell-Mann were not scientists at Los Alamos at the time.

The aspiration was to develop an institute where scientists could focus on problem-driven scientific research rather than paradigm-orientated science. The original focus of the institute was to propagate the concept of the new research field of complexity theory and related systems. Researchers work to understand and unify the underlying shared patterns in complex physical, biological, social, cultural, technological, and even possible astro biological worlds. The global research network of scholars spans borders, departments, and disciplines, unifying curious minds steeped in rigorous logical, mathematical, and computational reasoning.

SFI offers a wonderful free Community Lecture Series to the Santa Fe community with lively and diverse talks exploring cutting-edge research insights and the nature of human creativity and complexity.

* **The School for Advanced Research (SAR)** was originally founded in 1907 as a center for archaeological research. **It** is North America's preeminent independent institution advancing creative thought and innovative work in social sciences and humanities and fostering the preservation and revitalization of Native American cultural heritage. The school now has a global reach in social sciences and humanities scholarships. The school offers symposia, salons, classes, and field trips to meet and learn from their scholars and artists. It conducts leading-edge research and study in anthropology and related disciplines in order to foster a better understanding of humankind and the critical problems it faces.

SAR includes one of the most important collections of Southwest Native American art and helps guide museums around the world on best practices in collaborating with source communities. The Catherine McElvain Library at the School for Advanced Research (SAR) focuses on anthropology and Native American studies. The library archives document the programs, people, and history of SAR, including the Indian Arts Research Center. Archival materials relate to the twentieth-century history of Santa Fe, archaeology in the Southwest, and Native American art. The School for Advanced Research adopted its current name in 2007. From 1917 to 2006, it was known as the School of American Research. Before that, it was called the School of American Archaeology from its founding in 1907. The Indian Arts Research Center (IARC) is a division of SAR.

SAR offers symposia, salons, classes, and field trips that give a unique opportunity to meet and learn from SAR scholars and artists.

* **St. John's College (SJC)** is the third oldest college in the United States,

behind Harvard and the College of William and Mary. It is a private liberal arts school with campuses in Annapolis, MD, and Santa Fe. The university offers Bachelor of Arts and Master of Arts degrees in liberal arts on both campuses and a Master of Arts in Eastern classics at the Santa Fe campus.

St. John's is unlike most schools because students (or Johnnies, as students or alumni are called) share a common curriculum centered on reading and discussing some of the most important thinkers over the last 3,000 years. At the core of St. John's is a liberal arts curriculum focused on reading and discussing many of history's greatest books and most important questions. The classes lead students through the Great Books seminar style, with faculty facilitating active discussions. Every class is interdisciplinary discussions about the books are led by professors (or tutors, as they are called). It has a 7:1 student-faculty ratio, with every class less than 20 students. Students are required to take four semesters of language classes, including Ancient Greek and French, as they learn to translate classical texts. Students also study classical scientists and work to recreate their experiments through three years of laboratory science classes and two years of music study. The Santa Fe campus, in the foothills of the Rocky Mountains, has some of the best hiking, biking, and skiing trails in the US. Santa Fe is also home to more than 250 art galleries, great food, and live music. Frank Bruni, the New York Times columnist, described St. John's College as "The Most Contrarian College in America."

St. John's College hosts a free lecture series that is open to the public with a question-and-answer period. St. John's also has a Summer Classics program, a 30-year-old seasonal program in the spirit of lifelong learning. Summer Classics seminars are not lectures or book clubs; they are lively, in-depth, and highly participatory conversations on enduring works that span fiction and nonfiction, math and science, poetry and philosophy, and visual, cinematic, and performing arts.

♪ **Women's International Study Center (WISC)** "Inspires and enables women to achieve their goals" and was founded in 2013 to carry forward the legacy of the women of Acequia Madre House. WISC focuses on advancing the work and study of women in various fields, including arts, sciences, cultural preservation, business, and philanthropy. The center ensures that its programs are intergenerational, multicultural, and cross-disciplinary. WISC offers fellowships to provide opportunities for study, research, and collaboration to support women in their pursuit of knowledge and achievement.

Inspired by the women of Acequia Madre House and their work in the arts, sciences, cultural preservation, and business, WISC was founded to carry the women's legacy into the future through Fellowships related to these interests. The WISC Fellows-in-Residence program provides scholars, artists, authors, and others with residency in a fully furnished house to advance their work and engage with the community. To date, WISC has supported over 70 individual fellows from 7 countries, covering a vast range of topics and disciplines of local and global interest. WISC is located in the historic Acequia Madre House.

International Santa Fe
Santa Fe's 10 Sister Cities

- Bukhara, Uzbekistan

- Holguin, Cuba

- Icheon, South Korea

- Livingstone, Zambia

- Parral, Mexico

- San Miguel de Allende, Mexico

- Santa Fe de la Vega, Spain

- Sorrento, Italy

- Tsuyama, Japan

- Zhangjiajie, China

Santa Fe was the first United Nations Creative City in the United States and third in the world.

Chapter 10

PERFORMING ARTS

The Sound of Live Music, Theater, and Dance

Santa Fe Opera House

The Santa Fe Opera (The Crosby Theater) opened in 1957 and is the only open-air opera house in the United States. In 2023, 85,000 people attended the opera, with about half coming from outside New Mexico. It originally seated 480 but has grown to its present seating capacity of 2,126 and 106 standing-only. Its annual summer season runs from mid-June through August. Performances begin close to sunset so that the lighting of the productions is not compromised by the theatre being open to the outside environment.

Acoustics: Crosby chose the site for its natural acoustic properties. He worked with acoustician Jack Purcell to identify the ideal site on Crosby's 76-acre property that would serve as a sonic bowl. In 1997, the theater was rebuilt to include a fully covered, curved roof that created a "fullness" to the sound produced: Noise bounces off the curvatures of the wood ceiling in such a way that there are no acoustically bad seats.

Design: Three features distinguish the Santa Fe Opera from other opera houses. (1) scenery cannot be lowered from above (2) there is no proscenium arch that could support a curtain onto which surtitles could be projected; and lastly, (3) the sides are open, but the rear of the stage can also be completely opened to provide westward views.

Awards: Festival of the Year, International Opera Awards, Madrid, Spain (2022); Award for Excellence in Design, AIA/New York State (2000); USITT Award of Merit, United States Institute of Theatre Technology (1999), and Best Buildings Award, Exteriors Category, New Mexico Business Journal (1999)

First production: Puccini's *Madama Butterfly* was the first opera performed on July 3, 1957.

Fun to do: Arrive early to tailgate or at least to *look* at the tailgaters who are having way more fun than you are. You'll see gourmet meals complete with candelabra all the way to sandwiches. There is also a highly recommended buffet sit-down dinner available before the opera.

You might not know that Igor Stravinski helped bring attention and raise the public and professional profile of the Santa Fe Opera in its earliest years. For more than six years, the Santa Fe Opera put on some of Stravinsky's most famous operas, and Stravinski attended them all, including the first North American performance of *Persephone* in 1961. Look for Stravinski's bust on the Stravinsky Terrace.

History: Founder John O. Crosby first got to know the Santa Fe area because he spent time as a child at the Los Alamos Ranch School just outside Santa Fe. Much later, he returned to Santa Fe to find a place that would bring together live music and Santa Fe's "ideal climate, natural beauty, and [the] interest of the public in the great southwest." Crosby was a musician, conductor, and composer who came to New Mexico in 1943 for a cure for his chronic asthma.

Before Crosby and the opera theater, the land had been used as a pig farm and then a guest ranch.

In 1963, extensions and the two-story curved loggia were added to the stage roof.

On July 27, 1967, the theater was totally destroyed by fire during the premiere of Paul Hindemith's *Cardillac*. The Opera finished the season by performing in the Santa Fe High School gym, located on Marcy Street where the City of Santa Fe Tourism Center is located today.

After the fire, the theater was rebuilt to a new design with more seating and some weather protection. The new building expanded public spaces and improved the stage, backstage, and working spaces, but it was still open to the sky and weather.

In 1998, it was remodeled again to incorporate the Sangre de Cristo Mountains into the set design.

Trivia
The difference between opera and a musical?
In opera, music is more important than words.
In a musical, words are more important than music.

The Lensic Performing Arts Center

This is the heart and soul of Santa Fe's live music and performing arts scene hosting more than 200 events each year. It started in 1931 as a movie palace and was a hub for entertainment during the golden age of cinema. In 1925, the Atchison, Topeka, and Santa Fe Railway acquired the Lensic and leased it to Fred Harvey. The Lensic hosted music shows, dance performances, films, and lectures during the Fred Harvey era. In the late 1990s, the Lensic underwent extensive renovations to restore it architecturally and transform it into a state-of-the-art performing arts center. The nonprofit Lensic Performing Arts Center now owns and maintains the Lensic. Its mission is "to enrich lives by bringing diverse art and people together." It serves as a center for education, community events, and youth programs, offering accessible and affordable programming. Nearly 18,000 students benefit from its educational initiatives each year. The Lensic hosts a wide range of events, including concerts, theater productions, dance performances, lectures, and more. 211 W San Francisco St

Center for Contemporary Arts Santa Fe (CCA)

The Center for Contemporary Arts Santa Fe (CCA) is a community-supported arts center featuring the best in cinema, contemporary chamber music, immersive theater, contemporary art, and more. CCA offers a year-round schedule of activities and hosts many events each and every week. Several non-profits make CCA their Santa Fe home, including:

- **CCA Cinema** is Santa Fe's only independent, nonprofit cinema and one of the most popular theaters in Santa Fe. CCA Cinema curates exceptional, first-run independent and foreign films and documentaries featured on 2 screens (109-seat cinema and 49-seat cinema). CCA also curates several monthly film series, including:

  - **Closer Looks** (an examination of arthouse classics with post-screening discussions)

  - **Amplified** (a series that showcases music films and documentaries)

  - **Auteur** (a series of visionary film works that exists on the margins of the industry)

- **Chatter** Every Saturday morning at CCA, Chatter presents a contemporary chamber music concert at 10:30 am in the CCA Muñoz Waxman Gallery. The program includes one hour of music curated by Chatter Artistic staff and spoken word presented by a guest poet or writer.

- **The Exodus Ensemble** Several days each week, The Exodus Ensemble presents contemporary, immersive theatre productions in the CCA Spector-Ripps Gallery. Exodus creates explosive, original adaptations of classics where live theatre, cinema, and audience interaction collide. Exodus Experiences are rated Theatre-MA and are appropriate for audiences 18+. Exodus includes a company of 13+ professional actors based at CCA.

- **Tia Collection**: is a global art collection with a mission to support artists and museum institutions by acquiring and loaning works of art. Through its lending program, partner exhibitions, and publications, Tia aims to foster dialogue, stewardship, and scholarship of art. Tia curates a bi-monthly exhibition of art in the CCA Muñoz Waxman Gallery, and each installation is curated by the Tia team to share insight into the different perspectives we all experience with art.

Jean Cocteau Cinema

Jean Cocteau Cinema (418 Montezuma Avenue) is an eclectic art-house theater owned by author George R. R. Martin. It is a great venue for a diverse range of events, including:

- Film Screenings: From older classics to contemporary films.

- Variety Shows

- Comedy Shows

- Author book signings

- Q&A sessions with directors and authors

The Santa Fe Symphony Orchestra & Chorus

It is the only professional symphony orchestra with chorus in Northern New Mexico. It includes 65 professional musicians, all New Mexico residents, and a volunteer chorus of over 70 singers. The season runs from September through May, presenting 10 to 12 subscription concerts at the historic Lensic Performing Arts Center, free community performances at the Cathedral Basilica of St. Francis of Assisi, plus special events and chamber performances at unique venues across Santa Fe. The Santa Fe Youth Symphony Association is merging with the Santa Fe Symphony.

Santa Fe Chamber Music Festival

The Santa Fe Chamber Music Festival is a six-week-long summer festival of chamber music held annually in July and August. It was founded in 1972, with its first concert series in 1973, and now attracts both local and international audiences.

The festival has more than 90 internationally renowned musicians and ensembles performing during the festival, featuring 45 concerts, including classical, world premieres, and relative unknowns. Concerts take place in various venues, including the St. Francis Auditorium inside the New Mexico Museum of Art, and The Lensic, a historic theater in downtown Santa Fe.

Santa Fe Desert Chorale

Founded in 1982, the Santa Fe Desert Chorale is a 24-voice group that is one of the longest-running professional music organizations in New Mexico. It is also one of the most distinguished American professional chamber choirs, made up of professional choral singers from across America.

The Chorale's annual Summer Festival, held in July and August, is one of the nation's largest choral events, and for 10 days in December, the Chorale performs holiday music. The concerts are held in the Basilica of St. Cathedral Francis of Assisi. Each year, they host an annual community singing workshop, Santa Fe Sings, and the Chorale provides *the homeless in Santa Fe access to music* through its *Hearts in Harmony* program at the Interfaith Community Shelter. Through its *Insights & Sounds* program, the Chorale also presents free mini-concerts to introduce children to choral music.

Pro Musica

Founded in 1980, Santa Fe Pro Musica offers a variety of classical music programs in historic Santa Fe venues, including an Orchestra Series in the Lensic Performing Arts Center, a String Quartet Series presenting world-renowned string quartets in St. Francis Auditorium, and the Loretto Chapel Series featuring chamber music on historical instruments. Pro Musica has achieved a GRAMMY nomination, a 5-year affiliation with the Smithsonian Institution, and national recognition for its decades-long support of women in leadership roles in classical music. https://sfpromusica.org/

Performance Santa Fe

Performance Santa Fe brings the very best of music, dance, and theater to iconic Santa Fe locations. Alongside its extensive performance season, PSF runs three dynamic, exciting, and inclusive educational programs for students in the community— Arts for Life, the Masterclass Series, and the Field Trip Series. Santa Fe's longest-running performing arts organization invites you to experience world-class music, dance, and theater. Today, PSF offers a robust 10-month season of exceptional music, dance, and theater alongside its award-winning education. https://performancesantafe.org/

Live Music Venues

- Club Legato (in Café Sena) 125 E Palace Ave
- Cowgirl BBQ (319 S Guadalupe St)
- El Farol (808 Canyon Road) every Friday and Saturday evenings at 6:30 pm
- El Flamenco Spanish Cabaret (135 W. Palace Ave.) Friday and Saturday dinner starts at 6:15 pm and shows start at 7:30 pm.
- Evangelo's Cocktail Lounge (200 W San Francisco)
- Hilton Buffalo Thunder (20 Buffalo Thunder Trail)
- La Fiesta Lounge in the La Fonda Hotel (100 E San Francisco St)
- Meow Wolf (1352 Rufina Circle)
- Social Kitchen + Bar (725 Cerrillos Rd)
- Tiny's Restaurant & Lounge (1005 S. St. Francis Dr)
- Tumbleroot Brewery & Distillery (2791 Agua Fria St)

Aspen Santa Fe Ballet

The Aspen Santa Fe Ballet has two performance branches: (1) Aspen Santa Fe Presents and (2) Aspen Santa Fe Ballet Folklórico. The ballet company also has a ballet school. All ballet performances are performed at the Lensic Theater (211 W. San Francisco Street)

Theater Santa Fe

Theatre Santa Fe brings together the best of Santa Fe's live performance companies. Theatre Santa Fe was founded to foster collaboration, creativity, and community among local theater artists and enthusiasts. Theatre Santa Fe is the umbrella organization www.theatersantafe.org

Theater Companies
(from their websites)

Blue Raven Theatre produces original female-centric comedies and dramas. www.blueraventheatre.com/

Capital High School's Theatre Arts and Film Department offers multiple classes in Theatre Arts and Film Classes. All performances are in the Bryan Fant Theatre, a 350-seat proscenium arch theatre with a full fly system modified thrust stage and orchestra pit. The theatre is located on the Capital High School Campus. www.theatresantafe.org/capital-high-school-theatre-department

Family Theatre of Santa Fe provides engaging, quality theatre experiences for diverse multi-generational families. https://familytheatresantafe.org/

Incite Shakespeare Company Santa Fe (ISC) "engages and builds community through imaginative, entertaining, and insightful performances, using Shakespeare as a mirror to reflect our time." They perform in the Ensemble Summer Rep season and as a change of pace, the Bar(d) Speak Easy Shakespeare at different Santa Fe breweries and local bars. https://iscsantafe.org/

Ironweed Productions produces plays rooted in the American experience. Ironweed is committed to utilizing the vast, eclectic talent within Northern New Mexico, cultivating young and emerging theater artists, and cooperating with other performing arts organizations to support and promote live theater. www.ironweedsantafe.com/

Just Say It Theater allows the young people of Santa Fe to experience the magic and power of theater by writing and publicly performing their own collaborative theater pieces. www.justsayittheater.com/

LiveArts Santa Fe is a performing arts organization that provides accessible and equitable performing arts experiences in Santa Fe. Their mission includes various aspects of the arts, including youth programs, roaming cabaret events, and revitalizing the Greer Garson Theater Center. www.liveartssantafe.org/

New Mexico Actors Lab performs six plays during May, August, September,

October, and November. 1213 Parkway Drive. www.nmactorslab.com/

New Mexico School for the Arts is the only four-year, statewide public high school serving artist-scholars across New Mexico with a rigorous, award-winning pre-professional arts and academics program. NMSA provides students in 9th through 12th grades with intensive, pre-professional instruction in five major arts disciplines: Creative Writing and Literature, Dance, Music (voice or instrumental), Theatre, and Visual Arts. www.nmschoolforthearts.org/

Pandemonium Productions produces musicals that enrich the lives of young people through performing arts. Its Musical Theatre Program provides an equal focus to theater, dance, and music and the development of skills and knowledge in each of these performance disciplines. www.pandemonium-prod.org/

Santa Fe High School Theater nurtures young artists in the various elements of production, performance, and analysis. It produces an average of five full productions a year. Students involved in the department perform in main stage productions of both "straight" and "musical" shows, student-directed productions, state theater festivals, solo performance pieces, and world premieres. www.santafehigharts.com/

Sant Fe Classic Theater Santa Fe Classic Theater is a professional, non-profit theater company that presents and promotes the works of classic playwrights, from Sophocles to Shakespeare to Simon, for multicultural audiences in New Mexico. It is a professional company committed to the highest standards of excellence in theater. Santa Fe Classic Theater produces *Shakespeare in the Garden* at Santa Fe Botanical Garden. www.santafeclassictheater.org/

Santa Fe Playhouse (https://santafeplayhouse.org/) is a non-profit professional theater founded in 1919 by American novelist and essayist Mary Hunter Austin as The Santa Fe Little Theatre. It holds the distinction of being "the oldest continuously running theater west of the Mississippi." The playhouse hosts plays, musicals, and other performances, providing entertainment and artistic experiences for locals and visitors alike. 142 East De Vargas Street https://santafeplayhouse.org/

Teatro Paraguas stages contemporary award-winning Latinx plays in English and bilingual productions of Hispanic/Latinx poetry and classic folk tales while promoting children's theatre, producing the works of New Mexico playwrights, and celebrating the history, richness, and diversity of New Mexico's many cultures and artistic talent. www.teatroparaguasnm.org/

Theater Grottesco creates a new kind of visual, explosive, and full of surprise performance. The Grottesco Ensemble performs live performance by juxtaposing classical and modern theatrical styles with a daring, poetic research of culture and imagination, giving voice to the marginal elements of our contemporary society and taking audiences to the brink of emotional wonder and soulful reflection. www.theatergrottesco.org/

Tri-M Productions brings a variety of musical theater shows to Santa Fe while providing opportunities for talented young adults to continue to perform in their lives. www.trimsantafe.org/

Upstart Crows of Santa Fe is a Shakespeare troupe for young people 10 - 18. They produce workshops and uncut plays with a focus on understanding and collaboration. The Crows also perform the works of George Bernard Shaw and Oscar Wilde, have a dramatic reading troupe that performs Dickens' Christmas Carol each December, and host an adult reading group that closely reads plays that the youth troupe is performing. www.upstartcrowsofsantafe.org/

Wise Fool Circus Arts welcomes adults and teens of all ages, genders, sizes, fitness, and experience levels for ongoing classes in circus arts. You'll find fun and engaging classes, knowledgeable instructors offering after-school programs, week-long summer camps, and year-round classes that include stilt-walking, unicycling, aerial fabric, trapeze, juggling, puppet-making, clowning, and more! https://wisefoolnewmexico.org/

Theater Venues

(from their websites)

The Actors Lab (1213-B Parkway Drive) has flexible seating on risers for up to 110 seats; a professional light board; basic sound system and board; front and rear projection systems; sprung floor; a cafe space with a counter, microwave, and large fridge; two bathrooms; two dressing rooms; a lobby; Wi-Fi; and plenty of free parking. www.nmactorslab.com/

International Shakespeare Center (3209-A Calle Marie) can be set up as a rehearsal space, dance space, for informal theatre productions, in a seminar setting with chairs and tables, in the round, or lecture style. It has a lobby with a check-in desk, a conference table, a microwave, a coffee machine, a tea kettle, and space for setting up food. The main space is about 1066 square feet (approximately 35 x 30) with a sprung floor. It has windows that open, heating, air conditioning, floor fans, two couches, a bathroom, a water fountain, about 70 chairs, 10 tables, fast Wi-Fi, and lots of free parking. https://iscsantafe.org/

Santa Fe Playhouse (142 E. De Vargas Street) is the oldest continuously running theatre west of the Mississippi, establishing Santa Fe as a quality, engaging theatre destination. https://santafeplayhouse.org/

Teatro Paraguas (3205 Calle MarieTeatro) promotes literature and theatre through English, Spanish, and bilingual presentations of contemporary Hispanic and Latino poetry and plays while promoting children's theatre, producing the works of New Mexico playwrights, and celebrating the history, richness, and diversity of New Mexico's many cultures and artistic talent. www.teatroparaguasnm.org/

Chapter 11

HIGHLY OPINIONATED FOOD AND DRINK AND MORE

LET'S EAT!

Subjectively, the most popular foods associated with Santa Fe

- Biscochito
- Christmas burrito
- Frito pie
- Green chile cheeseburger
- Green chile stew
- Posole
- Sopaipillas
- Tamales

> **Chili and Chile –**
> **What's the difference?**
> Chile refers to a hot *pepper*
> Chili is a *food dish*

What's the big deal with green chiles?

First, the green chili is truly a New Mexico food. The chiles range from 200 to 7,000 in Scoville heat units. A green chile will ripen into a red chile. Green chile can be a plant, a sauce, a spice, or a stew. Second, they taste great.

OK. Now, what's the big deal with *Hatch* Green Chile?

It's named after the town of Hatch in New Mexico, which seems reasonable. Hatch is the only region where they grow, with a short season, only from August to September. They are almost always roasted because raw chiles taste pretty rough while roasting transforms them into a unique sweet and smoky taste. They usually come in either mild, medium, or hot; with the hot being like a trip to Bombay hot!

Now, what's the big deal with Chimayo Chile pepper?

Chimayo is a small village just north of Santa Fe that is known for the Chimayo chili pepper. It is usually only grown in very small batches and is hand-picked, so it is expensive and sells out quickly.

Green Chile Cheeseburger Trail

The trail has many locations serving green chili cheeseburgers throughout the state. These include the Atrisco Café & Bar, La Plazuela at the La Fonda Hotel, the Burger Stand at Burro Alley, and Tune-Up Café in Santa Fe; the Mine Shaft Tavern in Madrid; and Bob's Burgers in Albuquerque.

Want to feel the burn?

Horseman's Haven is known for its hot (seriously hot) green chile sauce. Its name comes from St. Michael's High School sports team, the Horsemen. Why one is horse*men* and the other is horse*man* is an unexplainable phenomenon. It's open Tuesday from 8:00 a.m. to 2:00 p.m.; Wednesday, Thursday, and Friday from 8:00 a.m. to 7:00 p.m.; Saturday from 8:00 a.m. to 7:00 p.m.; and Sunday from 8:30 a.m. to 2:00 p.m. 4354 Cerrillos Rd.

Best Restaurants (2023)

AAA

- Tia Sophia's
- Café Pasqual's
- The Shed
- Maria's New Mexican Cuisine
- Geronimo
- The Compound Restaurant
- El Farol
- Coyote Café & Rooftop Cantina
- Chocolate Maven Bakery & Café
- Cowgirl Bar and Grill
- Upper Crust Pizza
- Gabriel's

Conde Nast

- Geronimo
- The Shed
- Sazón
- Tia Sophia's
- Jambo Café
- The Compound
- Kakawa Chocolate House
- La Boca
- El Chile Toreado
- Dolina Bakery & Café
- Horno Restaurant
- Paloma

Fodor's

- Arroyo Vino
- Café Pasqual's
- Dolina Café & Bakery
- El Nido
- Fire & Hops
- Geronimo
- Harry's Roadhouse
- Joseph's Culinary Pub
- La Boca and Taberna
- La Choza

Gayot

- La Boca
- Compound
- Dinner for Two
- Restaurant Martin
- Geronimo

- La Casa Sena
- Santacafé
- Terra
- 315 Restaurant & Bar

Travel Awaits

- Restaurant Martin
- 315 Restaurant & Wine Bar
- Izanami
- Sassella
- Rio Chama Steakhouse
- La Boca
- Café Pasqual's
- El Farol
- Sazon
- Geronimo
- Santa Café
- Coyote Café & Rooftop Cantina
- Dinner for Two

Travel + Leisure

- Geronimo
- Compound
- Tia Maria's
- The Pantry
- Kakawa Chocolate House
- Dolina Café and Bakery

Tripadvisor

- Geronimo
- Sassella
- Sazón
- The Ranch House

- Dolina Bakery & Café
- Market Steer Steakhouse
- Clafoutis
- Paper Dosa
- Jambo Café
- Pantry Restaurant
- Palacio Restaurant
- Plaza Café Downtown

Yelp

- The Shed
- Pantry Restaurant
- Sazon
- Geronimo
- Cafecito
- El Callejon Taqueria and Grill
- Tomasita's
- Rowley Farmhouse Ales
- The Ranch House
- Mille

Personal favorites

Breakfast

- Café Fina
- Clafouti's
- Counter Culture
- Henry and the Fish
- La Plazuela at La Fonda
- Mille
- Palacio Cafe
- Red Enchilada

- Sunrise

Lunch and Dinner

- Cafecito
- Cowgirl
- Harry's Roadhouse (American comfort food)
- Konami (Japanese)
- La Plazuela at the La Fonda Hotel (New Mexican)
- Los Potrillos (Mexican)
- Saigon Café (Vietnamese)
- Sweetwater Harvest Kitchen (healthy)
- Vinaigrette (salads and sandwiches)

Special Occasion

- Compound
- Coyote Café & Rooftop Cantina
- Geronimo
- Izanami at Ten Thousand Waves

Happy Hour

- Bishops Lodge
- Cowgirl
- Dinner for Two
- El Farol
- Hotel Eldorado
- The Living Room at The Inn and Spa at Loretto

For insider information, check out Santa Fe foodies
https://santafefoodiesnm.com/

Guy Fieri Visits Santa Fe

- Jambo 2023
- Tune-Up Café, 2009

- Joseph's Culinary Pub, 2023
- Rowley Farmhouse Ales, 2021
- Rancho Plaza Grill, 2023
- Bert's Burger Bowl 2021
- Arable, 2019

James Beard Award

- Best Chef (2024) Eduardo Rodriguez, Zacatlán, Finalist
- Outstanding Restaurant (2024) The Compound, Finalist
- Best New Restaurant (2024) Alkemē, Semifinalist
- Best Chef Southwest (2023), Luis Medina El Chile Toreado, Semifinalist
- Best Chef Southwest (2023) Berenice Medina, El Chile Toreado, Semifinalist
- Best Chef Southwest (2023) Horno Restaurant, David Sellers, Semifinalist
- Best Chef (2022), Ahmed Obo, Best Chefs, semifinalist, Jambo Café
- Best New Restaurant (2022) Zacatlán Restaurant, Semifinalist
- Best Chefs (2022), Fernando Olea, Sazón, Winner (2022)
- Best Chefs (2018), Martin Rios, Restaurant Martin, Nominee (2018)
- Rising Star Chef of the Year (2018), Colin Shane, Arroyo Vino, Semifinalist
- Rising Star Chef of the Year (2017), Colin Shane, Arroyo Vino, Semifinalist
- Best Chefs (2017), Martin Rios, Restaurant Martin, Nominee
- Best Chefs (2016), Andrew Cooper, Terra at the Four Seasons Resort Rancho Encantado, Semifinalist
- Best Chefs (2015), Andrew Cooper, Terra at the Four Seasons Resort Rancho Encantado, Semifinalist
- Best Chefs (2015), Martin Rios, Restaurant Martin, Nominee
- Best Chefs (2014), Martin Rios, Restaurant Martin, Semifinalist
- Best Chefs (2014), James Campbell Caruso, La Boca Semifinalist
- Best New Restaurant (2014), Izanami at Ten Thousand Waves,

Semifinalist

- Best Chefs (2013), James Campbell Caruso, La Boca Semifinalist
- Outstanding Service (2013), The Compound Restaurant, Semifinalist
- Best Chefs (2013), Martin Rios, Restaurant Martin, Nominee
- Best Chefs (2012), Martin Rios, Restaurant Martin, Semifinalist
- Outstanding Service (2012), The Compound Restaurant, Semifinalist
- Outstanding Service (2011), The Compound Restaurant, Semifinalist
- Best Chefs (2011), Martin Rios, Restaurant Martin, Semifinalist
- Best New Restaurant (2010), Restaurant Martin, Semifinalist
- Best Chefs (2010), James Campbell Caruso, La Boca, Semifinalist
- Best Chefs (2010), Eric DiStefano, Coyote Café, Semifinalist
- Outstanding Service (2010), The Compound Restaurant, Semifinalist
- Best Chefs (2008), James Campbell Caruso, La Boca, Semifinalist
- Newspaper Feature Writing with Recipes (2008), Ronni Lundy, 'At One with Bees', Nominee
- Best Chefs (2008), David Sellers, Amavi, Semifinalist
- Best Chefs (2005), Mark Kiffin, The Compound Restaurant, Winner
- Best Chefs (2004), Mark Kiffin, The Compound Restaurant, Nominee
- America's Classics (2003), The Shed, Winner
- Best Chefs (1999), Katharine Kagel, Café Pasqual's, Nominee
- America's Classics (1999), Café Pasqual's, Winner
- Outstanding Restaurant Graphics (1996), Mike Fink, The Double A, Winner
- Best Chefs (1996), Mark Miller, Coyote Café, Winner
- Best Chefs (1991), Mark Miller, Coyote Café, Nominee
- Who's Who of Food & Beverage in America (1985), Tom Margittai,

Winner

⌇ Who's Who of Food & Beverage in America (1984), Mark Miller, Winner

Santa Fe Reporter Best of 2023

Best Artisan Chocolate: Kakawa Chocolate House
Best Asian Restaurant: Izanami
Best BBQ: The Ranch House
Best Bread: Sage Bakehouse
Best Breakfast: Clafoutis
Best Burger: Santa Fe Bite
Best Cakes: The Chocolate Maven
Best Catering: Walter Burke Catering
Best Cocktails: Coyote Cantina
Best Coffee: Iconik
Best Croissants: Clafoutis
Best Desserts: The Chocolate Maven
Best Fine Dining: Geronimo
Best Food Truck: Fusion Tacos
Best Frozen Treat: La Lecheria
Best Gluten Free: Sweetwater Harvest Kitchen
Best international Cuisine: Paper Dosa
Best Italian Restaurant: Piccolino
Best Local Distillery: Santa Fe Spirits
Best Locally Brewed Beer: Santa Fe Brewing Company
Best New Mexican Restaurant: La Choza
Best New Restaurant: Dumpling Café
Best Patio: Harry's Roadhouse
Best Pizza: Back Road Pizza
Best Steak: The Bull Ring
Best Tea: The Teahouse
Best Vegetarian: Jambo Cafe

The First Food Truck (maybe)

What just might have been the first food truck was the chuck wagon that was invented by Colonel Charles Goodnight. He was a cattleman who, in 1866, prepared to drive a herd of 2,000 longhorns from Texas to Colorado. Since it would be a long trip without the luxury of towns along the way, Goodnight had the idea of rebuilding an Army surplus wagon. He equipped it with cabinets, cubbies, shelves, and drawers to hold food, utensils, a hinged worktop for meal prep, and a large water barrel on the side. There was also space for bedrolls, blankets, and slickers.

Since the cowboys referred to their meals as "chuck," (an English term that referred to good, hearty food), this invention became known as the chuck wagon. It became popular and was copied throughout the West. The Studebaker Company and others began producing chuck wagons and selling them for the very expensive price of $100. The long cattle drive era only lasted about 20 years and peaked in the 1880s. But archive photos show cowboys out on the open range cooking and eating at the chuck wagon as late as the 1930s.

Best Food Trucks According to Yelp (2023)

- El Chile Toreado
- Fusion Tacos
- Bang Bite Filling Station
- Santafamous Street Eats
- Il Encanto
- Saya's Frybread & Indian Tacos
- Sanchez Tacos
- Bo's Authentic Thai
- Santa Fe Kitchen
- Lupe's Andale 2
- Albuquerque Journal Best Food Trucks In Santa Fe (2023)
- Fusion Tacos
- Santafamous Street Eats
- Lupe's Andale
- Ras Rody's Jamaican Vegan
- El Queretano
- El Chili Toreado
- Taqueria Gracias Madre
- Sanchez Tacos

Get Cooking with Cooking Schools

- Eatwith
- Las Cosas Cooking Classes
- Open Kitchen
- Red Mesa Cuisine
- Santa Fe School of Cooking. Throughout the year, they add a little spice when the school transforms into Dave's Jazz Bistro to host terrific jazz dinners with world-class jazz musicians. Terrific. Don't miss.

LET'S DRINK!

Traditional Toast

"Salud, amor y pesetas, y tiempo para disfrutarlas"
(Health, love and money, and time to enjoy them)

Maybe the Most Famous Santa Fe(ish) Cocktail

(Chimayo is about 28 miles from Santa Fe)

The **Chimayo cocktail** was invented by Arturo Jaramillo, the owner of the Rancho de Chimayo restaurant in Chimayo, New Mexico in 1965. The recipe is:

1.5 ounces tequila
1-ounce unfiltered apple cider
¼ ounce fresh lemon juice
¼ ounce crème de cassis over ice

Taos Lightning

Original recipe: whiskey, red pepper, black gunpowder, tobacco juice
The Taos Lightning was the preferred drink of mountain men and fur trappers (and maybe because it was the *only* drink available). It was probably single-handedly responsible for much of the drunkenness and lawlessness of the old West from the 1830s to 1847 when the owner, Simon Turley, was killed in the Taos Revolt. Legend has it that Peg Leg Smith, a mountain man and trapper got his name when he was shot in the knee that became so infected his leg had to be amputated. Peg Leg Smith took a few drinks of Taos Lightning and did the amputation himself.

Taos Lightning has been brought back by KGB Spirits with hopefully, a little less potency.

Happy Hour!

- Agave at the El Dorado Hotel (4:00 pm-6:00 pm daily)
- Andiamo! (4:30-6:00 pm daily)
- Chile Line Brewery and Lino's Trattoria and Pizzeria (3:00 pm-6:00 pm daily)
- Cowgirl BBQ (3:00 pm-6:00 pm Monday-Friday)
- Dinner for Two (*4-6:30 pm and 8:30-10*)
- Eldorado Hotel and Spa (Agave Restaurant and Lounge 4:00 pm-6:00 pm daily)
- El Farol (3:00 pm-5:00 pm daily)
- Hidden Mountain Brewing Co (3:00 pm-6:00 pm Wed-Fri)
- La Boca (3:00 pm-5:00 pm, Wed-Sat)
- Osteria D'Assisi Ristorante Italiano (4:30 pm-6:00 pm daily)
- Pranzo Italian Grill (4:00 pm-6:00 pm daily)
- Rio Chama (3:00 pm-5:00 pm, M-F)
- SkyFire at Bishop's Lodge (2:00 pm-5:00 pm Monday-Friday)
- Terra at Four Seasons Rancho Encantado (3:00 pm-5:00 pm daily)
- The Living Room, Inn and Spa at Loretto (4:00 pm-6:00 pm daily)
- The Ranch House (3:00 pm-6:00 pm daily)
- Vanessie Restaurant and Bar (4:00 pm-6:00 pm Thursday-Monday, closed Tuesday and Wednesday)

Breweries

- Beer Creek Brewing Co. 3810 HWY 14
- Desert Dogs Brewery & Cidery Taproom 112 W. San Francisco Street
- Hidden Mountain Brewing 4056 Cerrillos Road
- Leaf & Hive Brew Lab 1208 Mercantile Rd
- New Mexico Hard Cider Tap Room 505 Cerrillos Road
- Nuckolls Brewing Co. 430 W. Manhattan
- Paxton's Taproom 109 N. Guadalupe St

- Rowley Farmhouse Ales 1405 Maclovia St.
- Santa Fe Brewing Company multiple locations
- Santa Fe Spirits 7505 Mallard Way Unit 1
- Second Street Brewery 2920 Rufina Street and the Railyard
- Tumbleroot Brewing & Distilling 2791 Agua Fria Street

Coffee Roasters

- 35 Degrees Coffee Roasters
- Iconik Roasters
- Odd Box Roasters
- Ohori's Roasters

Coffee? You Want Coffee? We Got Coffee!

Opens 6:30 am to 7:00 am

- Starbucks 6:30 am - 6:30 pm everyday
- Betterday Coffee 7:00 am-5:00 pm everyday
- Downtown Subscription 7:00 am-4:00 pm everyday
- Dutch Brothers 5:00 am -10:00 pm Sunday-Thursday, 5:00-11:00 Friday and Saturday
- Java Joe's 7:00 am-1:00 pm Monday-Saturday, closed Sunday
- The Mud Hut by Agapao Coffee 7:00 am-5:00 pm Monday-Saturday, Sunday 7:00-3:00 pm
- New Baking Company 7:00 am to 3:00 pm every day
- Ohori's Coffee Roasters 7:00 am-6:00 pm Monday-Saturday, 9:00-3:00 pm Sunday
- Palace Coffee and Tea 7:00 am-3:00 pm Wednesday-Monday closed Tuesday
- Tribes Coffee House 7:00 am-5:00 pm daily

Opens at 7:30 am

- 35 North Coffee 7:30 am-4:30 pm everyday
- Baked and Brew 7:30 am-2:00 pm Monday-Friday
- Cake's Café & Coffee Shop 7:30 am-4:00 pm Sun-Th, 7:30-7:00

Friday and Saturday

- Iconik Coffee Roasters and Café 7:30 am-5:00 pm everyday
- CrashMurderBusiness 7:30 am-3:00 pm M-F, 9:00 am-3:00 pm Saturday, closed Sunday

Opens at 8:00 am

- Craft Donuts and Coffee 8:00 am-2:00 pm M-F, 8:00 am-1:00 pm Sat, Sunday closed
- Madame Matisse 8:00 am-3:00 pm W-Sun, closed Monday & Tuesday
- Modern General Feed and Seed 8:00 am-4:00 pm every day
- Sky Coffee 8:00 am-3:00 pm everyday

Opens at 9:00 am

- Travel Bug 9:00 am-5:00 pm M-Sat, Sunday noon-4 pm

Opens 11:00 am or after

- Boba Tea Company 11:00 am-8:00 pm M-Th, 10:00 am-8:00 pm Friday and Saturday, noon-6:00 pm Sunday
- The Good Stuff Café Vinyl, Café & Coffee Shop 11:00 am-6:00 pm every day
- Remix Audio Bar, Café & Coffee Shop 1:00 pm-6:00 pm Tuesday-Saturday, closed Sunday and Monday

Margarita Trail

The Margarita Trail includes specialty margarita drinks at 52 participating locations. To participate, download the app 'Santa Fe Margarita Trail Passport'. Present your app for $1 off the signature margarita offered at each participating location. Ask the bartender to "stamp" your app. Once you get a minimum of 5 stamps, you can redeem them for merchandise at the Downtown Santa Fe Visitor Center at 66 E. San Francisco Street, Suite 3.

Margarita Trail Downtown Santa Fe locations:

- Agave Lounge
- Amaya at Hotel Santa Fe
- Anasazi Restaurant, Bar & Lounge
- Boxcar

- Bull Ring
- Club Legato at La Casa Sena
- Cowgirl BBQ
- Coyote Café & Rooftop Cantina
- Del Charro Saloon
- Dinner for Two
- Dr. Field Goods
- Dragon Room Bar at the Pink Adobe
- El Farol
- Joe's Tequila Bar
- Kitchen + Bar at the Drury
- La Choza
- La Fiesta Lounge in La Fonda on the Plaza
- Living Room at the Inn & Spa at Loretto
- Low n' Slow Lowrider Bar and Lounge
- Maria's New Mexican Kitchen
- Ortiz Restaurant & Bar at Hilton Santa Fe Historic District
- Osteria D'Assisi Ristorante Italiano & Piano Lounge
- Palace Prime
- Rio Chama
- Secreto Lounge
- Social Kitchen + Bar at The Sage Hotel
- Staab House Bar at La Posada
- The Alley, Lanes + Lounge
- The Compound Restaurant
- The Plaza Café – Downtown
- The Shed Restaurant
- Thunderbird Bar & Grill
- Tomasita's Restaurant
- FLOAT Café & Bar at Meow Wolf

- Hidden Mountain Brewing
- La Reina at El Rey Court
- The Plaza Café – Southside
- The Ranch House
- Tortilla Flats Restaurant
- Tumbleroot Brewing and Distilling

Out a ways:

- The Bourbon Grill
- Cottonwood Kitchen
- El Nido
- Harry's Roadhouse
- Izanami Restaurant
- Iguana Café/Red Sage at Buffalo Thunder
- Mine Shaft Tavern
- Rancho de Chimayo Restaurante
- SkyFire at Bishop's Lodge, Auberge Resorts Collection
- Terra Bar at Four Seasons Resort Rancho Encantado

PROBABLY TMI

The Easy Peasy (not!) 12-step Application Process for a Liquor License in New Mexico

The Liquor Control Act does not allow convicted felons to own or be an officer on a Liquor License, so fingerprinting is required to receive background reports from the state and federal levels. The application process takes approximately 4 to 5 months.

1. Preliminary review of application
2. Posting Request sent to Department of Public Safety, done by Special Investigations Unit;
3. Notice of Preliminary Hearing – must be held within 30 days of receipt of your application.
4. Notice of Publication – The Applicant is required to publish notice of the hearing, at least 72 hours in advance of your hearing, in a local newspaper of general circulation.

5. Notice of Deficiencies – lists the items necessary to correct or complete your application.
6. At Preliminary Hearing – This is a public hearing to read the application into the record.
7. Issuance of Hearing Officers Recommendations
8. Review of Recommendations by the Director for Preliminary Approval
9. Application forwarded to Local Option District
10. Decision by Local Option District
11. Notice to Applicant of Final Deficiencies
12. Final Approval by the Director

Oh, you want to open a restaurant *with* a liquor license?
No problem (not!)

Restaurant Licensee hours are from 7:00 am until 11:00 pm or when food service stops, whichever is earlier.

These are the *additional* Restaurant License Requirements

⌁ A license cannot be issued to an establishment serving only soups, salads, sandwiches, and other fast foods.

⌁ A menu must be submitted showing hours and days of operation.

⌁ Only a full-service restaurant whose primary function is the sale and service of food will qualify for this type of license.

⌁ Must have a commercial kitchen and the employees necessary for preparing, cooking, and serving food.

⌁ Pictures of your establishment are required including the kitchen, prep, dining, alcohol storage, and patio areas.

⌁ To qualify for Renewal of a Restaurant License, at least 60% of the gross receipts must come from the sale of food and no more than 40% may come from the sale of alcohol.

⌁ A Restaurant A License is non-transferable from person to person or from location to location.

⌁ A Restaurant B license is nontransferable from person to person but may transfer from location to location within the same local option district.

New Mexico State Statute allows for the addition of sales and service of spirituous liquor under the Restaurant License. Here are the new types:

1. Restaurant A, for beer and wine only
2. Restaurant A+ for New Mexico Produced Spirits only
3. Restaurant B, for beer, wine, and any spirit

Also enacted is the ability to sell and deliver alcoholic beverages with a minimum $10.00 order of food. A current restaurant licensee will need to obtain an Alcohol Beverage Delivery Permit. The requirements are:

- The purchase must be made at the establishment and delivery must be made within the normal, authorized business hours.
- To be delivered by an employee, 21 years of age or older, who holds a current Server Permit and valid driver's license.
- A third-party delivery service may also be used.

Chapter 12

NATIVE AMERICANS
AND
SANTA FE

A LITTLE BACKGROUND: HOW WE GOT HERE

Citizenship. Before 1924, Native Americans were not US citizens. It took the Indian Citizenship Act of 1924 for Native Americans to become citizens. The Act stated that all Native Americans born in the United States were granted citizenship, but this act did not ensure full citizenship rights, such as the right to vote because of arguments based on the "Indians not taxed" clauses.

Voting. Even though a high percentage of Native Americans served in World War II, they were not allowed to vote, even though they had served in the military. In 1948, Miguel Trujillo, a WWII Marine veteran, schoolteacher, and member of the Isleta Pueblo wanted to vote, but the county registrar Eloy Garley refused to allow him to register. Trujillo took Garley to court and sued for the right to vote resulting in the case, Trujillo v. Garley.

Like several other western states, New Mexico held that "Indians not taxed" could not vote. Trujillo challenged this by pointing out that although he did not pay property taxes since he lived on Pueblo lands, he still paid federal income, gasoline, and sales taxes. The three-judge panel in Albuquerque ruled in Trujillo's favor and found that the provisions in the New Mexico constitution violated both the Fourteenth and Fifteenth Amendments.

Indian Removal and the Reservation Period (1829-1886) Beginning in the early 19th century US governmental policies removed Native people from their homelands and forced them to live in abject poverty on Reservations. By the late 19th century 90% of North American Indians had perished because of these policies, diseases for which they held no immunities, and warfare. However, some tribal groups of the Southwest, such as Pueblo and Navajo Indians were ultimately able to remain in their original homelands.

The Long Walk (1864-1865) was the result of the US government forcing the Navajo people to move from their homeland between 1864 and 1868. This was forced on them as punishment for resisting U.S. expansion policies.

Major General Carleton ordered Christopher (Kit) Carson to stop Navajo resistance through a scorched-earth campaign. Carson burned villages, slaughtered livestock, and destroyed water sources, forcing the Navajo to surrender.

After the surrender, the U.S. military marched approximately 9,000 Navajo men, women, and children between 250 to 450 miles, depending on the route, from Fort Canby in Arizona to Bosque Redondo Reservation in New Mexico, with about 500 dying on the way. This 'walk' took about 3 weeks through winter conditions, with the Navajo carrying only the clothes on their backs. The journey was arduous, and the weaker individuals who could not keep up with the military pace were often either left to die or shot. In all, nearly 2,500 Navajo died either on the journey or in the terrible conditions at the destination of Bosque Redondo. By November 1864, about 8,570 people were imprisoned there.

When they arrived at Bosque Redondo, they found that it could not be farmed, and the only water came from the Pecos River, which had alkali, causing dysentery. Because trees were being rapidly used for building as well as firewood, they had to travel over 20 miles for firewood. Other factors were that the Navajo were placed next to the Mescalero Apache, who they didn't get along with, and they were also close to the Comanches, who raided the unarmed Navajo. All these factors meant that the Navajo faced starvation, disease, and death.

While at Bosque Redondo, the US expected that the Navajo (Diné) would embrace American cultural values, such as Christianity, individualism, and the English language, especially through their children. This policy was often referred to as the federal Indian assimilation policy.

As the Navajo (Diné) faced worsening conditions, news of the internment camp spread with photographs depicting their misery and suffering. U.S. officials visiting the camp could see that there were not enough resources to care for the Navajo. By 1866, Carson ordered that no more prisoners be sent to Bosque Redondo.

Navajo oral history recounts the terror inflicted by Carson's men, who showed no regard for women, children, or families. Finally, the Navajo Treaty of 1868 reversed their removal, allowing them to return home. The Long Walk had a major impact on the Navajo culture and identity, and it remains an important part of their history.

Note: The Long Walk is about the Navajo (Diné), while the Trail of Tears is about the Cherokees, a different tragedy.

The Navajo Nation Treaty of 1868 holds historical significance as a pivotal agreement between the United States and the Navajo Nation, allowing them to return to their ancestral lands and maintain their culture and sovereignty. The key points in the treaty:

- Both parties pledged to cease all hostilities with the U.S. government committed to maintaining peace.

- The treaty defined the Navajo reservation boundaries and recognized the sovereignty of the Navajo Tribe within these lands.

- An agent was assigned to oversee Navajo affairs, and compulsory education for Navajo children was established.

- Individual land allotments were provided with seeds and agricultural implements supplied.

- The treaty allowed for railroads, military posts, and roads to cross the reservation.

- Attacks on U.S. citizens or their property were prohibited.

- Conditions for validating future treaties were outlined.

- The reservation became the permanent home for the Navajo people.

Assimilation Policies (1887-1932) included the establishment of boarding schools. U.S. government officials removed young children from their homes and discouraged or forbade Native children from speaking their languages and practicing religious ceremonies. Many Native adults were encouraged to learn a trade or farming techniques, all of which contributed to diminishing Native cultures and languages.

Tribal Sovereignty. These constitutional provisions and subsequent interpretations by the Supreme Court can be summarized in three principles of U.S. Indian law:

- **Territorial sovereignty**: Tribal authority on Indian land is organic and is not granted by the states in which Indian lands are located.

- **Plenary power doctrine**: Congress, not the Executive Branch or Judicial Branch, has ultimate authority over matters affecting Indian tribes. Federal courts give greater deference to Congress on Indian matters than on other subjects.

- **Trust relationship**: The federal government has a "duty to protect" the tribes, implying (and courts have found) the necessary legislative and executive authorities to effectuate that duty.

Santa Fe Indian School

The Santa Fe Indian School (SFIS) was established in 1890 to educate Native American children throughout the southwest. The federal government established the school during the Boarding School era for the purpose of assimilating native children. This was done by removing Indian children from their community and prohibiting them from practicing their native language and beliefs. By this separation of their cultural and individual identities, the children could adopt new standards for living the American way of life.

In 1933, the Bureau of Indian Affairs was established and charged with protecting the Native Americans. American Indians in New Mexico boarding schools thrived, creating a 180-degree shift in Indian education.

In 2000, with the signing of the Santa Fe Indian School Act, the land was turned over to be held in trust for the 19 Pueblo Governors of New Mexico. This allowed SFIS to build a program based on educational sovereignty—the right and responsibility to educate New Mexico Indian children in a manner that supports their cultural and traditional belief systems. The program teaches 7th through 12th grades.

Native Americans on the Plaza

The Native American Artisans Portal Program, run by the Museum of New Mexico, showcases traditional Native American work. It has worked to protect and promote traditional southwestern Native American arts and crafts since 1909. By museum policy and legal rights, the portal of the Palace of the Governors has been reserved for Native Americans to display and sell crafts made by themselves or members of their households.

The Program encourages buyers to interact with artisans who display their handmade crafts under the portal of the Palace of the Governors. Vendors are members of 23 federally recognized Native American tribes, pueblos, or nations located within New Mexico. The only exceptions are spouses of New Mexico Native Americans who are *themselves* enrolled members of Native American groups outside New Mexico, and graduates of Santa Fe's Institute of American Indian Arts in Santa Fe.

As part of the application process, each of the 1,500 artisans currently authorized to participate in the Portal Program have all demonstrated technical mastery of their craft. On a typical day, 68 vendors display their handmade art and crafts.

Eight Pueblos North of Santa Fe

TESUQUE PUEBLO (10 miles from Santa Fe)
www.tesuquecasino.com
Te-Tsu-Geh (Tewa) "Cottonwood Tree Place"

Tesuque Pueblo has been in its present location since 1680 and is listed on the National Register of Historic Places. Although Tesuque is one of New Mexico's smallest pueblos with only about 400 people living there, it includes 26 square miles in the Sangre de Cristo Mountain foothills. The Pueblo was founded in 1694 with farming being the primary economic engine. Tesuque Pueblo artists create traditional work including pottery, bead jewelry, painting, and sculptures, particularly rain gods, small pottery figures originally created for tourists in the 1880s. However, today, the artisans are making them with pride and the figurines are sought after collectibles.

Must see:
Tesuque Casino
- Tesuque Pueblo Flea Market
- Saturday Corn Dance and Blessing of the Fields (June 1)
- San Diego Feast Day (November 12)

POJOAQUE PUEBLO (15 miles north of Santa Fe)
www.pojoaque.org
P'o Suwae Geh (Tewa) "Water Gathering Place Village"

War and disease nearly demolished Pojoaque Pueblo but residents returned in the 1930s. The residents evicted squatters, erected fences, and rebuilt. Today the Pueblo is thriving thanks partly to its Poeh Cultural Center and Museum, which provides a wide range of art instruction, demonstrations, and world-class exhibitions of contemporary and traditional art and culture. 100 of its ancient pots were returned from the Smithsonian National Museum of the American Indian (although temporarily).

The Pueblo operates one of the state's largest luxury resorts, featuring fine dining, golf, and spa services, along with two casinos. The Hilton Santa Fe Buffalo Thunder Resort & Casino also displays one of the largest collections of museum-quality Native American Fine Art in the state.

Must see:

- ♪ Farmer's Market (weekly)
- ♪ Bison Range (tours by appointment only)
- ♪ Three Kings Day Celebration (January 6)
- ♪ Our Lady of Guadalupe Feast Day honoring the Pueblo's patron saint (December 12)

NAMBÉ PUEBLO (18 miles north of Santa Fe)
www.nambepueblo.org
Nambe (Tewa) "People of The Round Earth"

Nambé Pueblo's history dates back to the 1300s when it played a pivotal role as a center of culture and religion. Because of its importance as a social and economic hub, the Spanish conquerors that began arriving in the late 16th century tried to destroy it and nearly succeeded. Today, Nambé is known for traditional pottery, jewelry, and sculpture and also for its beautiful location in the Sangre de Cristo Mountains where a spectacular double-drop waterfall, a lake, and a campground make up the popular Nambé Pueblo Recreation Area. The Pueblo has strong agricultural traditions, a buffalo range, and offers tours arranged in advance.

Must see:

- ♪ Celebration at Nambé Falls (4th of July weekend)
- ♪ Easter Sunday Dances (Evening Firelight Vespers) (Easter Sunday weekend)
- ♪ St. Francis de Assisi Annual Feast Day (October 4)
- ♪ Buffalo Dance Following Christmas Eve Mass) (December 24)

SAN ILDEFONSO PUEBLO (23 miles north of Santa Fe)
www.sanipueblo.org
Po-Who-Ge-Oweenge (Tewa) "Where the Water Cuts Through"

Between 1200 and 1500 A.D., early residents of San Ildefonso Pueblo left Mesa Verde in Colorado and Chaco Canyon to settle on the Pajarito

Plateau in the present-day Bandelier National Monument. Due to drought, they relocated to their current location near the Rio Grande and towering Black Mesa in the late 1500s or early 1600s—and it was from this mesa top that Pueblo residents fought Spanish soldiers during the Spanish re-conquest of New Mexico in 1694.

San Ildefonso is home to many well-known artists, including the late renowned potter Maria Martinez and her husband, Julian. They developed their famous black-on-black polished and matte pottery introduced to the world by Maria at the 1904 World Fair in St. Louis. Many potters continue to create the black-on-black and also red style. San Ildefonso today remains a major arts community where visitors can purchase work directly from artists' homes in this flourishing community.

OHKAY OWINGEH PUEBLO (25 miles north of Santa Fe)
www.ohkay.com
Formerly San Juan Pueblo (Tewa) "Place of the Strong People"

When Juan de Oñate established the first Spanish capital city in New Mexico in 1598, it was on the land of Ohkay Owingeh Pueblo, formerly San Juan Pueblo, where there stands a plaque to denote this today. Po'Pay, a medicine man who lived at Taos Pueblo when he led the Pueblo Revolt in 1680, was born at Ohkay Owingeh. Today, Ohkay Owingeh is home to San Juan Lakes, a popular fishing spot, the Eight Northern Indian Pueblos Council, The Rio Grande runs through the Pueblo, which is surrounded by unusually tall trees.

Must see:

- Native Arts of the Rio Grande Gallery & Cooperative and the Ohkay Casino, Resort and Hotel
- Ohkay Owingeh St. John's Feast Day with Comanche and Buffalo Dances (June 23-24)
- Arts and Farmers Market every Saturday (July-October)
- Indian-Spanish hybrid Matachines Dance (December 24 & 25)
- Turtle Dance (December 25)

SANTA CLARA PUEBLO (28 miles from Santa Fe)
www.santaclaran.com
Kha'P'O (Tewa) "Singing Water Village"

Puye Cliffs was home to 1,500 Pueblo Indians who lived, farmed, and hunted game there from the 900s to 1580 AD. Then, due to drought circa 1550, the Puye Cliff Dwellers abandoned their homes, relocating to Santa Clara Pueblo, about 20 miles away. Today, Santa Clara artists such as world-renowned sculptor Roxanne Swentzell from the Naranjo potter family are acclaimed for their black and red polished pottery, including signature double-necked wedding jars and hand-molded black animal figures, as well as willow baskets, decorated gourds, and textiles.

Must see:

- Puye Cliff Dwellings Visitor Center & Museum (Native Dancers perform at the Visitor Center on the weekends)
- The Santa Claran Hotel & Casino
- Black Mesa 27-hole golf course
- St. Anthony's Feast Day features Comanche Dances (June 13)
- Santa Clara Feast Day with Buffalo, Harvest, and Corn Dance (August 12)

PICURIS PUEBLO (60 miles north of Santa Fe)
www.picurispueblo.org
Pinguiltha (Tiwa) "Mountain Warrior Place"

When Spanish colonist Juan de Oñate encountered the residents of this Pueblo more than 400 years ago, he named the Pueblo Pikuria, for "those who paint." Artistic traditions still flourish at Picuris, which is famous for micaceous pottery. Picuris Pueblo is nestled on the banks of the Rio Pueblo River where it sits in a serene spot known locally as "the hidden valley." Residents recently completed a major restoration by hand of their 200-year-old adobe mission church, San Lorenzo de Picuris.

Must see:
- Picuris Pueblo Visitor Center

- The Pueblo's bison herd
- Povi Fine Arts Gallery
- Feast Day with Comanche and Buffalo or Deer Dance (January 23)
- Early in March, Mountain Sheep Dance
- San Lorenzo Feast Day with dances, pole climbing and a foot race (August 10)
- Feast Day of the Nativity with Corn Dance (September 10)
- The Picuris Pueblo Museum where local art is displayed and sold
- Native-themed Hotel Santa Fe including the Hacienda & Spa featuring the Amaya Restaurant (in which the Pueblo holds a majority interest) in downtown Santa Fe and which offers tours to the Picuris Pueblo.

TAOS PUEBLO (68 miles north of Santa Fe and one mile from Taos)
www.taospueblo.com
Tau-Tah (Towa) "The Place of the Red Willows"

Taos Pueblo, with its world-famous, multi-storied adobe communal architecture set against the backdrop of Taos Mountain, is one of North America's oldest, continuously occupied villages. It is also a UNESCO World Heritage Site and a National Historic Site. Local artists sell from their family homes, some of which have been converted into mini-shops and galleries.

Taos Pueblo is located at the beginning of the eastern plains, served as a major trading center for centuries, and its Trade Fair drew thousands of mountain men, trappers and other traders. The Pueblo's artists are known for their micaceous clay pottery, jewelry, paintings, moccasins, and drums. Farming and seasonal ceremonies are key to traditional Pueblo life and Taos is one of the more active present-day Pueblo farming communities.

Must see:

- September 30 Feast Day of San Geronimo, with pole climbing and an arts and crafts fair
- 2nd weekend in July, Taos Pueblo Powwow brings together Indian Nations from across the country

Note about the languages: There are three separate dialects within the Tanoan language: Tewa, Tiwa, and Towa. Tiwa dialect is spoken in Taos, Picuris,

Sandia, and Isleta Pueblos. Tewa dialect is spoken in San Juan, Santa Clara, San Ildefonso, Nambe, Tesuque, and Pojoaque Pueblos. The Towa dialect is spoken only in Jemez Pueblo.

It wasn't until tribal elders realized that their languages were dying that they allowed language dictionaries to be made that would preserve their languages. Even though the people of Jemez Pueblo are the only speakers of Towa, they still forbid any written forms of their language effectively stopping any possible Towa Dictionary.

CASINOS

Casinos within 20 miles of Santa Fe

- Tesuque Casino (7 miles)

- Hilton Santa Fe Buffalo Thunder Resort Casino: largest casino in Santa Fe and northern New Mexico (15 miles)

- Cities of Gold Casino (17 miles)

Background of Casinos in Santa Fe

Unlike Tribal casinos in many other states, New Mexico's casinos are managed by the tribes themselves, keeping casino operations aligned with Tribal culture and social values. This is all subject to the oversight of the National Indian Gaming Commission, gaming compacts with the state, and the Indian Regulatory Act.

Indian gaming is based on the legal foundation of The U.S. Supreme Court case, California v. Cabazon Band of Mission Indians. This decision held that if state law criminally prohibits a form of gambling, then the tribes within that state may not engage in that activity. However, if state law civilly regulates a form of gambling, then the tribes within the state may engage in gaming free of state control.

America's Indian Reservations still have some of the highest rates of poverty, unemployment, and shortest life expectancies in the nation, which are being addressed with the help of casino revenues. By state law, the Pueblos' and Tribes' share of casino profits are to be used to fund community services, economic development projects, and Pueblo/Tribal government operations.

All of the gaming Pueblos/Tribes have used casino proceeds to fund housing, health care, and education services. As an example, Sandia Pueblo, which operates the State's largest casino, will send its members to any school, anywhere, free of cost.

The State of New Mexico also directly benefits from tribal gaming resulting in increased tax revenues, and since two-thirds to three-quarters of casino employees are non-native New Mexicans, payroll is spread beyond the tribes.

The Gaming Control Board (GCB) regulates gaming in the state, including the 22 New Mexico tribal casinos and five racetrack casinos. Tribal casinos may operate casino-style gaming, including slot machines and table gaming, while slot machines are allowed at racetrack casinos and licensed non-profit and fraternal organizations. The state collects money from gaming in two ways: revenue sharing from tribal casinos and taxing revenues from racetrack casinos and other licensed operators. In FY23, revenue from tribal casino revenue sharing was $241 million.

Native American Feast Days

Tribal members come together in celebration of their language, culture, and religion. The communities celebrating feast days are open to the public, and members of the tribe will prepare a variety of meals to share with guests.

Pueblo Etiquette

When visiting the Pueblos in New Mexico, it is essential to remember that these ancient communities have rich cultural traditions, and it is crucial to respect their rules and customs.

Each Pueblo operates under its own government and establishes rules for its village, so respect and abide by the laws and wishes of the specific Pueblo you are visiting.

While most Pueblos are open to the public during daylight hours, homes are private and should never be entered without an invitation.

Kivas (ceremonial rooms) and graveyards are sacred places restricted for use by Pueblo members only. Never enter unless invited.

Stay off walls and structures; some are several hundred years old and can be easily damaged.

Nature is sacred to the Pueblos.

Littering is strictly prohibited; dispose of trash properly.

On feast days and other public observances, enter a home by invitation only; but if you are invited, accept the invitation to eat, but don't linger, as your host will serve numerous guests throughout the day. After the meal, thank your host, but a payment or tip is not appropriate.

New Mexico Tribal Casinos

Source: 2019 New Mexico Legislative Finance Committee; New Mexico Racing Commission; Gaming Control Board

Name	Tribe	Slots	Table Games	Rooms
Apache Nugget	Jicarilla Apache	130	0	0
Black Mesa	San Felipe Pueblo	680	7	0
Buffalo Thunder	Pojoaque Pueblo	1,200	18	395
Casino Apache	Mescalero Apache	380	10	0
Cities of Gold	Pojoaque Pueblo	503	0	0
Dancing Eagle	Laguna Pueblo	600	0	0
Fire Rock	Navajo Nation	1,100	7	0
Flowing Water	Navajo Nation	130	0	0
Inn of the Mountain Gods	Mescalero Apache	840	35	273
Isleta Resort	Isleta Pueblo	1,743	34	201
Jake's Casino	Pojoaque Pueblo	63	0	0
Northern Edge	Navajo Nation	750	10	0
Ohkay Casino	Ohkay Owingeh	700	3	101
Palace West	Isleta Pueblo	261	0	0
Route 66	Laguna Pueblo	1,375	34	154
Sandia	Sandia Pueblo	2,300	38	228
Santa Ana Star	Santa Ana Pueblo	1,600	21	0
Santa Claran	Santa Clara Pueblo	680	6	122
Sky City	Acoma Pueblo	669	10	134
Taos Mountain	Taos Pueblo	200	4	0
Tesuque Casino	Tesuque Pueblo	800	10	0
Wild Horse	Jicarilla Apache	190	0	41

Chapter 13

MOVIES, TV SONGS AND BOOKS, OH MY!

Moviemaker Magazine ranked Santa Fe #1 among Best Places to Live and Work as a Moviemaker for 2023.

Movies Filmed in or about Santa Fe

- *3:10 to Yuma* (2007)
- *5 Shells* (2012)
- *A Gunfight* (1971)
- *The Avengers* (2012)
- *A Million Ways to Die* (2015)
- *All the Pretty Horses* (2000)
- *Americana* (2023)
- *And God Created Woman* (1988)
- *Appaloosa* (2008)
- *Begotten* (1989)
- *The Book of Eli* (2010)
- *Butch Cassidy and the Sundance Kid* (1969)
- *Carriers* (2009)
- *Cheyenne Social Club* (1970)
- *Corporate Animals* (2019)
- *Cowboys & Aliens* (2011)
- *Crazy Heart* (2009)
- *Dead For a Dollar* (2022)
- *Dead Man's Hand* (2023)
- *Deadman Standing* (2018)
- *Did you Hear About the Morgans?* (2009)
- *Easy Rider* (1969)
- *Fast Color* (2018)
- *Finch* (2021)
- *Georgia O'Keeffe* (2009)
- *Holiday in Santa Fe* (2021)

- *Hostiles* (2017)
- *Ideal Home* (2018)
- *In a Valley of Violence* (2016)
- *Legion* (2010)
- *Lightning Jack* (1994)
- *Little Treasure* (1985)
- *Milagro Beanfield War* (1988)
- *Natural Born Killers* (1994)
- *News of the World* (2020)
- *No Country for Old Men* (2007)
- *Odd Thomas* (2013)
- *Off the Map* (2003)
- *Oppenheimer* (2023)
- *Please Don't Feed the Children* (yet to be released)
- *Rattlesnake* (2019)
- *Rent* (2005)
- *Santa Fake* (2019)
- *Second Thoughts* (1983)
- *Seraphim Falls* (2006)
- *Terminator 2: Judgement Day* (1991)
- *The Harder They Fall* (2021)
- *The Homesman* (2014)
- *The Kid* (2019)
- *The Longest Yard* (1974)
- *The Magnificent Seven* (2016)
- *The Man from Laramie* (1955)
- *The Men Who Stare at Goats* (2009)
- *The Missing* (2003)
- *The Prodigal Planet* (1983)
- *The Tao of Steve* (2000)

- *The Vanishing of Sidney Hall* (2017)
- *Thor* (2011)
- *Those Who Wish Me Dead* (2021)
- *True Grit* (2010)
- *Twins* (1988)
- *Undead or Alive* (2007)
- *Where Angels Go, Trouble Follows* (1968)
- *Whiskey Tango Foxtrot* (2016)
- *Wild, Wild West* (1999)
- *Woman Walks Ahead* (2017)
- *Young Guns* (1988)

TV Series Filmed in or about Santa Fe

- *Breaking Bad* (2008-2013)
- *Dark Winds* (2022-2023, 3rd season coming)
- *Empire* (1962-1963)
- *Godless* (2017)
- *Lonesome Dove* (1989)
- *Longmire* (2012-2017)
- *Manhattan* (2014-2015)
- *Roswell, New Mexico* (2019-2022)
- *The Bachelor* (February 2, 2015)

Songs About Santa Fe

- "Santa Fe" by Bob Dylan
- "Airwaves" by Ray LaMontagne
- "Santa Fe" by Beirut
- "Amarillo by Morning" by George Strait
- "Santa Fe" by Adam Jacobs
- "Santa Fe" by Bon Jovi
- "Santa Fe" by the Bellamy Brothers

- "Here Comes the Santa Fe" by Riders in the Sky
- "The Santa Fe Trail" by Jolly Jack
- "The Santa Fe Trail" by Fair Annie
- "The Santa Fe Trail" by Ian Robb
- "Along the Santa Fe Trail" by Billy Corgan
- "Santa Fe" from the musical *Newsies*. Original key: D Major, vocal range: C#4 – A5
- "Santa Fe" by Jonathan Larson and Billy Aronson

Books Set in or About Santa Fe

- *A Bodkin for the Bride* by Patrice Greenwood
- *A Certain Malice* by Jake Page
- *A Dangerous Talent* by Charlotte Elkins
- *A Sprig of Blossomed Thorn* by Patrice Greenwood
- *A Spy's Guide to Santa Fe* and Albuquerque by E.B. Held
- *All I Ever Wanted* by Francis Ray
- *All of My Love* by Francis Ray
- *All That I Need* by Francis Ray
- *All That Remains* by Melva Haggar Dye
- *All the Stars in the Sky: The Santa Fe Trail Diary of Florrie Mack Ryder* by Megan McDonald
- *An Aria of Omens* by Patrice Greenwood
- *Biting the Moon* by Martha Grimes
- *Bless me, Ultima* by Rudolfo Anaya
- *Blood and Thunder* by Hampton Sides
- *Cazadora* by Julia DeBarrioz
- *Chasing the Cure in New Mexico: Tuberculosis and the Quest for Health* by Nancy Owen Lewis
- *Changing Spaces* by Nancy King
- *Commerce of the Prairies* by Josiah Gregg
- *Copper's Woman* by Carol Finch

- *Daughter Witch* by B. Austin
- *Death Comes for the Archbishop* by Willa Cather
- *Death of a Citizen* by Donald Hamilton
- *A Fatal Twist of Lemon* by Patrice Greenwood
- *Double Homicide* by Jonathan and Faye Kellerman
- *Drowning Cactus* by Carrie Russell
- *Dust Devel* by Parris Afton Bonds
- *Eagle Dancer* by Sharon Silva
- *Ed Eagle: Short Straw* by Stuart Woods
- *Extreme Denial* by David Morrell
- *Farolito Shadow* by PJ Christman
- *Finding Casey* by Jo-Ann Mapson
- *Fractal Despondency* by Trent Zelazny
- *Gardens of Santa Fe* by Anne Hillerman
- *Ghosts of the Black Rose* by Belinda V. Garcia
- *Girl in Pieces* by Kathleen Glasgow
- *Gossip Can Be Murder* by Connie Shelton
- *Gravity of Birds* by Tracy Guzeman
- *Husband and Wife Reunion* by Linda Style
- *Josefina Saves the Day: A Summer Story* by Valerie Tripp
- *Josefina: An American Girl* by Valerie Tripp
- *Joshua Croft Series* by Satterthwait
- *Just Josefina* by Valerie Tripp
- *Kings Lizard* by Pamela Christie
- *Lamy of Santa Fe* by Paul Horgan
- *Lemurian Medium* by G.G. Collins
- *Lightfall One: Clock, Cloak, Candle* by Jordan Taylor
- *Los Alamos* by Joseph Canon
- *Lost in a Room Full of Dinosaurs* by PJ Christman
- *Maxi Tex* by Claudio Nizzi

- *Mihael's Trial* by Serena Yates
- *Mothers and Other Liars* by Amy Bourret
- *Nina Otero-Warren of Santa Fe* by Charlotte Whaley
- *Nothing More and Nothing Less* by PJ Christman
- *Open Road* by M.J. O'Shea
- *Out of Agony* by Lynette Endicott
- *Protective Instinct* by Lynett Endicott
- *Rainbow's End* by Martha Grimes
- *Red Sky at Morning: A Novel* by Richard Bradford
- *Reluctant Medium* by G.G. Collins
- *Resurrecting Rain* by Patricia Averbach
- *Sailing an Alien Sea* by Cindy L. Gold
- *Santa Fe Dead* by Stuart Woods
- *Santa Fe Edge* by Stuart Woods
- *Santa Fe Rules* by Stuart Woods
- *Santa Fe Surrender* by Kristal Leigh Scott
- *Short Straw* by Stuart Woods
- *Skins of Lightning* by PJ Christman
- *Taos Chill* by Linda Castle
- *Tex Albo Speciale* by Mauro Boselli
- *The Return of Joy* by Lynette Endicott
- *The Anglo* by Jo Moore
- *The Blessing Way* (1ˢᵗ in the Leaphorn and Chee series) by Tony Hillerman
- *The Bone Fire* by Christine Barber
- *The Conquest of Don Pedro* by Harvey Fergusson
- *The Fiercest Star* by Julia DeBarrioz
- *The German Bride* by Joanna Hershon
- *The Gravity of Birds* by Tracy Guzeman
- *The King's Lizard* by Pamela Christie

- *The Looking Glass: Tales of Light and Dark* by H.L. Sudler
- *The Midnight Ride of Blackwell Station* by Mary Peace Finley
- *The Myth of Santa Fe* by Chris Wilson
- *The Road From La Cueva* by Sheila Ortego
- *The Shade of Santa Fe* by Eva Pohler
- *The Staircase* by Ann Rinaldi
- *The Trail to Santa Fe* by David Lavender
- *The Wind Leaves No Shadow* by Ruth Laughlin
- *Tularosa* by Michael McGarrity
- *Twin Seduction* by Cara Summers
- *Under the Color of Law* by Michael McGarrity
- *Under Witch Aura* by Maria E. Schneider
- *Wall of Glass* by Walter Satterthwait
- *Weekends with O'Keeffe* by CS Merrill
- *Where They Bury You* by Steven W. Kohlhagen
- *Winter in Taos* by Mabel Dodge Luhan

Chapter 14

BATTLES, WAR, REBELLIONS, MEMORIALS, AND BAD STUFF

Bataan Memorial Military Museum, New Mexico Military Museum

The Bataan Memorial Military Museum is located at 1050 Old Pecos Trail. Free admission.

Why in the world is the Bataan Military Museum in Santa Fe?

Because many of the American soldiers in Bataan were with the New Mexico National Guard, specifically the 200th and 515th Coast Artillery. Just before the start of WWII, the New Mexico National Guard was sent to the Philippines. On April 9, 1942, after months of constant battle, 75,000 United States and Filipino soldiers were forced to surrender to Japanese forces.

The soldiers faced horrifying conditions and treatment as POWs, deprived of food, water, and medical attention, and forced to march 65 miles to the POW camps. This march came to be called the Bataan Death March, where approximately 10,000 men died, including 1,000 Americans and 9,000 Filipinos. They would be prisoners of war until 1945, when U.S.-Filipino forces recaptured the Philippines.

Even after they were freed, about one-third of the prisoners died from health complications caused by the poor conditions at the POW camps; others were wounded or killed when unmarked Japanese ships transporting prisoners of war to Japan were sunk by U.S. air and naval forces. The deaths had a huge impact on New Mexican families. Of the 1,816 200th and 515th Coast Artillery men identified, 829 men lost their lives in battle, prisons, or after liberation.

Mormon Battalion Monument

31 miles South of Santa Fe, you'll see the Mormon Battalion Monument. The Mormon Battalion was the only religious unit in United States military history to be recruited solely from one religious body with a religious title as the unit designation. The volunteers served during the Mexican-American War (1846–1848) from July 1846 to July 1847.

Battle of Glorieta Pass

The battle took place in what is now Santa Fe County in 1862. Confederate forces wanted to take control of the mines, railroads, and cities throughout the area. This battle was the westernmost significant battle of the Civil War, ending the Confederacy's attempt to expand to the West. This battle represented the end of the Confederates' New Mexico campaign and it was an important event in New Mexico's Civil War history.

The battle began on March 26 with the main battle two days later on March 28. At first, the Confederates pushed the Union forces back through the pass but had to retreat when all their supplies were destroyed with the Union in full control by June. In all, there were about 375 casualties over the three days of fighting.

Pueblo Revolt 1680

Since the Spanish first conquered and colonized the Pueblos in 1598, the Pueblo people were forced to work under terrible conditions, often sold into slavery, and subjected to cruel punishment, with missionaries allowed to attack and suppress the Pueblo religion. On August 10, 1680, a medicine man from the San Juan Pueblo, Po'pay (Popé), led a coordinated revolt consisting of almost all of the Pueblo nations against the Spanish. This revolt was a big deal since each Pueblo was its own nation; getting them to work together was an incredible accomplishment for Po'pay. The Pueblo Revolt successfully overthrew Spanish rule but only lasted 12 years, when the Spanish reconquered the Pueblos in 1692, led by Governor Pedro de Vargas.

Texan Santa Fe Expedition

In 1841, the Republic of Texas wanted part of the trade conducted over the Santa Fe Trail but more importantly, Texas really wanted to annex the eastern half of New Mexico. This was a bit of a problem since it belonged to Mexico. The president of Texas, Mirabeau B. Lamar, had ambitions to make Texas into a continental power, which had to be accomplished quickly because there was a movement for Texas to be part of the United States, so he sent an expedition into New Mexico. This proved to be a big mistake because Lamar mistakenly believed that the New Mexicans would want to join the Republic of Texas. They did not.

The expedition was a total failure, with historian David Lavender calling it "one of the most cockeyed ventures in American history." The 320 Texans surrendered to the New Mexican governor Manuel Armijo and were marched 2,000 miles south to Veracruz, Mexico. They were released in 1842. After this expedition, Texans rejected Lamar and turned to Sam Houston, who wanted Texas to be part of the United States, which happened in 1845.

Bad Stuff in Santa Fe

Japanese Internment camp.

During WWII, the federal government ordered a Japanese American internment camp to be established with the Casa Solana internment camp established in March of 1942, when it held over 4,500 Japanese immigrant men, making it one of America's largest prison camps in the United States during WWII. The site also held German and Italian nationals.

New Mexico voted against interning any New Mexican citizens of Japanese heritage, so none of the Japanese New Mexicans were interned during WWII. Located on a hill at the Frank S. Ortiz Park in Santa Fe, NM, you can find a stone marker, placed there in 2002, commemorating the Santa Fe Internment Camp (SFIC).

The Obelisk or The Soldiers' Monument

This monument has been a source of intense controversy here for years. During the late nineteenth century, the monument, located on the Plaza, was used for annual Memorial Day events, a place for Union veterans to gather, decorate the cenotaph, and hear brief presentations. The square plinth included four inscribed panels, three of which memorialized Union soldiers from New Mexico who died in the battle of Glorieta Pass during the Civil War. The fourth panel memorialized US soldiers who died "in the various battles with savage Indians." The word "savage" was chiseled off anonymously in 1974 and on October 12, 2020, Indigenous People's Day, the obelisk portion of the monument was toppled by protestors. Today, on the Plaza, you'll just see the plinth, a base with nothing to display.

New Mexico State Penitentiary riot

The penitentiary is just south of Santa Fe. The riot took place February 2 & 3, 1980, when rioters held 12 guards hostage. At the time, the riot was the most violent prison riot in US history, lasting 36 hours, with 33 inmates dead and more than 200 injured. Many reasons led to the riot, including overcrowding (1,156 inmates with 963 beds), unsanitary conditions, failure to separate first-time non-violent prisoners from repeat violent prisoners, poor quality food, and the cancellation of educational, recreational, and other rehabilitative programs.

Santa Fe Ring

The Santa Fe Ring began in the 1850s controlling most of the local politicians. The ring included almost all state politicians in Santa Fe who had near total control of the state during the late 19th and early 20th centuries. The Ring realized that wealth could be achieved by owning or controlling the millions of acres of land that the Spanish and Mexican governments of New Mexico had granted to individuals and communities. The Ring was greatly helped by U.S. courts, which were unfamiliar and unsympathetic to Hispanic land practices, which had allocated most land grants to the first settlers and their descendants. The Ring obtained titles to the disputed Spanish and Mexican land grants by legal means and secured control of these lands for speculation. According to legend, the rerouting of U.S. Route 66 to avoid Santa Fe and go through Albuquerque was done to punish the Ring at the request of Governor Hannett.

$121.5 million Santa Fe Archdiocese settlement in New Mexico clergy sex abuse scandal

The archdiocese covers central and northern New Mexico and was established in the 1850s after the Mexican-American War. Some 74 priests have been deemed "credibly accused" of sexually assaulting children while assigned to parishes and schools by the archdiocese. An estimated $52 million has been paid in out-of-court settlements to victims in previous years. The Archdiocese of Santa Fe filed for Chapter 11 bankruptcy in 2018.

Zorro Ranch

This ranch included Jeffrey Epstein's infamous 26,700-square-foot house, which was one of Epstein's sites of alleged sexual coercion of children. It is the largest house in Santa Fe County and is located about an hour's drive south of Santa Fe on Highway 41.

Chapter 15

GET
OUTSIDE!

Santa Fe Botanical Garden

Opened in 2013, the garden is in Museum Hill with 20.5 acres divided into three sections: The Orchard Gardens, Ojos y Manos (Eyes and Hands), and the Piñon-Juniper Woodland.

The Orchard Gardens combines horticultural and architectural elements with plants selected for their beauty and ability to thrive in the Santa Fe landscape.

Ojos y Manos (Eyes and Hands) is an ethnobotanical garden featuring raised beds for annual crops and an extensive collection of plants with traditional uses.

The Piñon-Juniper Woodland is a 1/3-mile nature trail loop with great vistas of New Mexico's Mountain ranges. The Woodland provides for the conservation of a particular piñon-juniper woodland environment. In addition, this area provides a natural setting for discovery, contemplation, and movement along meandering trails. The Botanical Garden is open every day from 9:00 am-5:00 pm from April to October and 10:00 am to 4:00 pm from November to March.

A Few of the Hiking Trails

Atalaya Mountain is a 6.2-mile out-and-back trail, generally considered a challenging route, taking an average of 3 hours and 40 min to complete.

Arroyo Hondo is a 1.8-mile loop trail, generally considered an easy route, taking an average of 48 minutes to complete.

Big Tesuque Trail Alltrails.com says this is an easy 3.6-mile loop trail that takes an average of 1 hour and 40 minutes to complete. Dale Ball Trails include over 20 miles of trails, including the North Loop Trail, a 3.1-mile loop that takes around 1 hour and 18 minutes to complete. Dale Ball Trails can be accessed off Hyde Park Rd., Cerro Gordo Rd., Upper Canyon Rd., and Camino Cruz Blanca. Dogs are fine on a leash.

Dale Ball Trails are a network of 22 miles of hiking and mountain biking trails of interconnected paths, providing a range of options for various skill levels. The trails are well-maintained and clearly marked, making navigation relatively straightforward. The network includes a variety of routes, from gentle paths suitable for beginners to more challenging, steep climbs and descents for experienced hikers and bikers. There are also options for shorter loops or longer, more extensive outings, allowing visitors to tailor their adventure to their preferences and abilities. Many of the trailheads are easily accessible from various points in Santa Fe, making them popular destinations close to the city. Despite being so close to Santa Fe, the trails offer an escape from the hustle and bustle of daily life. Overall, the Dale Ball Trails offer a great opportunity to experience Santa Fe's nature while enjoying outdoor activities such as hiking, trail running, and mountain biking.

Galisteo Basin Preserve is a 6.4-mile loop trail near Lamy. It is generally considered a moderately challenging route, taking an average of 2 hours and 23 minutes to complete.

The Nature Conservancy's Santa Fe Canyon Preserve is just before the Audubon Center, where Upper Canyon meets Cerro Gordo. It is the trailhead for the 22-mile Dale Ball Trail network. The Preserve's 525 acres of open space includes the Bosque, which is a good area for birdwatching. A 1.5-mile loop details the site's history and ecology. The Dale Ball Trails are a cooperative effort between the city, county, the Foothills Trails Trust, and private landowners and has proven to be very popular with hikers and cyclists.

Santa Fe Baldy Starting at the Windsor trailhead, Alltrails.com says it will take about 7 and ½ hours to complete the 13.5-mile hike out and back. Oh, and it has a 3,464 feet elevation gain just to make it more interesting.

Santa Fe River Trail is a 2.4-mile out-and-back trail that takes an average of 47 min to complete. Dogs must be on a leash. Pick it up at De Vargas Park.

Sun Mountain is a 1.6-mile out-and-back trail that is generally considered a challenging route; it takes an average of 1 hour and 14 minutes to complete.

Upper Canyon Loop Trail is a 3.3-mile loop trail that takes an average of 1 hour and 46 minutes to complete. Interpretive signs located along the trail provide information on the history of the preserve and the important role it played in Santa Fe's water supply. There are multiple trailheads. The trail is for pedestrian use only. No dogs or bikes.

Running

Santa Fe Striders puts on several races every year, including the Santa Fe Snowshoe Classic, La Corrida de los Locos, the Santa Fe Run Around, the Santa Fe Striders Running Festival, and the Big Tesuque Trail Run. www. Santafestriders.org

Endurance Santa Fe puts on several races each year, including the "Ultra Santa Fe", and "Frozen Feb FatAss", an 8-mile nighttime trail run. www. endurancesantafe.com

Bicycling

- **Arroyo Chamiso Trail** runs along the Arroyo Chamiso channel, offering cyclists a peaceful and scenic route. It connects various neighborhoods in southern Santa Fe and provides access to parks, open spaces, and residential areas.

- **Gallisteo Basin Preserve** is located south of Santa Fe and features a network of trails, from easy loops to challenging routes in rugged terrain, where you can enjoy great views of the Galisteo Basin.

- **La Tierra Trails** offers a whole network of mountain biking trails with varying difficulty levels. These trails wind through juniper and pinon hillsides for both leisurely rides and more challenging rides.

- **Santa Fe National Forest Trails** are located to the east of the city with many trails that wind through pine forests and high desert landscapes.

- **Santa Fe Rail Trail** is a multi-use trail that follows the route of the old Atchison, Topeka, and Santa Fe Railway line, stretching approximately 17 miles from Santa Fe to Lamy. The trail is relatively flat and well-maintained, making it OK for cyclists of all abilities. It passes through scenic landscapes, including meadows, arroyos, and rural areas.

- **White Mesa** (about 52 miles away). According to Santa Fe's Broken Spoke Bicycle Shop, riding the trail at White Mesa "is worth the drive to discover one of the strangest, but beautiful, and fun rides in New Mexico. The trail is a network of rocky outcrops, smooth single track, and exotic colors" and takes about an hour to complete.

Pickleball

Pickleball is everywhere! Public play is available at Fort Marcy (indoors with fee and outdoors), Romero Park, Salvador Perez Park, and Genoveva Chavez Community Center

Ski Santa Fe

Just 16 miles away from Santa Fe, the Santa Fe Ski Basin has a base elevation of 10,350 feet and a peak elevation of 12,075 feet. It has 86 trails (20% easy, 40% intermediate, 40% expert), 37 of which are groomed daily. The annual snowfall is 225 inches with seven lifts.

Wildlife

Coyotes can be your friend. As Dan Flores in The New Mexican Magazine said, "Unlike the iconic bison, whose origins lie in Asia, the coyote emerged in the American Southwest 5.3 million years ago. All the world's wolves, jackals, dingoes, wild dogs, and our family pets had their beginnings right here, millions of years ago. But unlike most of them, coyotes come from a line of canids that never left America. Unlike coyotes, wolves migrated across the land bridges to much of the world, where they continued to evolve before returning to this continent 30,000 years ago."

Prairie dogs can be found throughout Santa Fe. The prairie dogs that you see are probably the Gunnison Prairie Dog. They have bigger hands and feet, shorter tails, and larger noses than the other four breeds of prairie dogs which helps them dig through clay-packed soils in hot desert environments. They live in colonies called "coteries." They are intelligent mammals with a complex "language" of more than 500 recognizable sounds.

They are mostly herbivores, although some eat insects. You can often hear their high-pitched "bark", which, of course, gave them their name. Prairie dogs are considered a keystone species, meaning that other animals rely on them to survive. When they dig and drag plants into their burrows and go to the bathroom underground, they fertilize the soil, helping more plants to grow and creating homes for insects, birds, and other wildlife. Even when prairie dogs move, their old burrows provide shelter for other animals, including rattlesnakes, jackrabbits, and burrowing owls. With deep networks of tunnels, water is able to seep deep into the ground, preventing erosion and water loss.

When winter is coming, they eat as much as they can to add an extra layer of fat, then go into their burrows to sleep. Some species of prairie dogs hibernate through the winter, while others only spend days at a time sleeping in a state, called torpor (a state of physical or mental inactivity or lethargy). Prairie dogs in torpor have lower body temperatures, heart rates, and breathing rates, just like in hibernation, but are active for a few hours every week instead of all winter.

Santa Fe is one of two places within the normal habitat of the Gunnison prairie dogs where they are officially protected.

Prairie Dog Pals (www.prairiedogpals.org) is an all-volunteer nonprofit dedicated to the welfare, preservation, and continuous humane treatment of urban prairie dogs.

People for Native Ecosystems (https://prairiedogpne.org/) protects, nurtures, and maintains Santa Fe's imperiled population of Gunnison's Prairie Dogs as they are vital links in the native ecosystem.

Note: It is legal to own prairie dogs as pets in New Mexico, Connecticut, Florida, Indiana, Minnesota, Mississippi, Montana, Nebraska, Nevada, North Carolina, Ohio, Oklahoma, Pennsylvania, South Dakota, Tennessee, Texas, Vermont, West Virginia, and Wisconsin.

New Mexico Wildlife Center (NMWC)

NMWC was founded in 1986 by a local veterinarian, Dr. Kathleen Ramsay. Originally formed as a rehabilitation center for injured birds, the organization has evolved to treat all wildlife species in New Mexico. NMWC is located at 19 Wheat Street in Espanola and is open for visitors Tuesday through Sunday from 9:00 a.m. to 4:00 p.m.

Flora, Fauna, Parks, and Other Green Things

- ⌇ Bicentennial Park (1121 Alto St)
- ⌇ Cathedral Park (213 Cathedral Pl)
- ⌇ DeVargas Park (302 W DeVargas St)
- ⌇ Entrada Park (50 Via Punto Nuevo)

- Fort Marcy Park (490 Bishops Lodge Rd)
- Frank S. Ortiz Park (160 Camino de Las Crucitas)
- Frenchy's Field (2001 Agua Fria St)
- Harvey Cornell Rose Park (1320 Galisteo Pkwy)
- Hillside Park (617 Paseo de Peralta)
- Hyde Memorial State Park (740 Hyde Park Rd)
- Las Acequias Park (1100 Calle Atajo)
- Patrick Smith Park (1010 E Alameda St)
- Pueblos del Sol Park (intersection of Governor Miles Road and Nizhoni Drive)
- Ragle Park (2530 West Zia Rd)
- Railyard Park and Plaza (740 Cerrillos Rd)
- Villa Linda Park (4246 W Rodeo Rd)

Professional Sports Teams, uh, Team

Santa Fe Fuego is a local baseball team that is very entertaining to watch with high scores, often scoring 20 or more runs in a game. Games are played at Fort Marcy Ballfield and start in May with tickets for $9. The team started in 2012 as part of the Pecos League, which is a professional league that plays to win championships, not develop players.

The closest professional minor league baseball team is the Albuquerque Isotopes, a Triple-A affiliate of the Colorado Rockies.

Santa Fe's Rodeo (Rodeo De Santa Fe) was started in 1949 and is held annually in June with over 500 cowboys and cowgirls competing.

The Santa Fe Roadrunners were a North American Hockey League team, but they moved to Kansas and became the Topeka Roadrunners.

Horse Racing was held at The Downs in Santa Fe from 1971 until 1997.

Trains and Planes

Rail Runner Express is a commuter railroad that goes from Santa Fe to Albuquerque to Belen. New Mexico Rail Runner has a fleet of nine MP36PH-3Cs and 22 Bombardier Bi-Level cars. While the engines are capable of 110 miles per hour, the track limits the maximum speed to 79 miles per hour. The one-way ride from Albuquerque to Santa Fe on the Rail Runner Express takes approximately 1.5 hours, runs seven days a week, except for some holidays, and goes from Downtown Albuquerque to Santa Fe Depot between three and eight times per day. With 15 stations along the Rail Runner's 100-mile corridor and more than 60 bus connections at those stations, the train offers a convenient schedule year-round and any day of the week.

Sky Railway Adventures: (text from Sky Railway)

- **Sunset Serenade**: Climb aboard for a magical sunset train ride in Santa Fe. Enjoy live entertainment while taking in the majestic desert sights. Duration: 2 - 2.5 hours.

- **Speakeasy Express**: Step into the swingingest joint on two rails! If you "speak easy" the password, you'll be treated to live music and 1920s cocktails. Duration: 2 - 2.5 hours.

- **Margarita Rail**: New this year! Sky Railway's nod to the famous Santa Fe Margarita Trail. Sip margaritas, enjoy amazing views, and groove to live music. Duration: 2 - 2.5 hours.

- **DeathCookie: A Murder Mystery**: Solve the murder of Leb Borkin and uncover the secret of "The Metamorphosis" on this sinister Sci-Fi journey. Duration: 2.5 - 3 hours.

- **Santa Fe Scenic**: Take in the beauty of New Mexico from restored passenger cars. Some trips include Native American hoop or buffalo dancing. Duration: 2.5 - 3 hours.

- **Lore of the Land**: Explore the Galisteo Basin while storytellers entertain you with New Mexico's history, complemented by live music. Duration: 2.5 - 3 hours.

- **New Mexico Wine Train**: Uncork the best wineries in New Mexico while enjoying gorgeous views. Duration: 2.5 - 3 hours.

- **Sky Railway Cab Rides**: The ultimate VIP experience, including one-on-one interaction with the operating crew. Ride the rails in style! Duration: 1 - 1.5 hours.

Amtrak serves the Santa Fe area generally. To catch an Amtrak train, you've got to go to Lamy Station in the town of Lamy, about 14 miles southeast of Santa Fe or can go to Albuquerque.

The Santa Fe Municipal Airport is the second busiest commercial airport in New Mexico, behind only the Albuquerque International Sunport. It first opened in 1942 and is undergoing Phase One of a much-needed airport improvement plan to improve the parking lot, expand the terminal, and re-model the existing terminal. It has 3 runways: Runway 2/20 is 8,366' x 150 ft, Runway 15/33 is 6,316' x 100', and Runway 10/28 is 6,301' x 75'.

- American Airlines provides regional jet service to Dallas/Fort Worth International Airport and Phoenix Sky Harbor International Airport.
- United Airlines has regional jet service to Denver International Airport and Houston Intercontinental Airport.

Chapter 16

I'M SO PRETTY

Awards, Kudos, Accolades, Superlatives, & Honors

US Postage Stamps Related to Santa Fe

- Palace of the Governors, 1¼ cent stamp (1946)
- Stephen Watts Kearny Expedition, "Capture of Santa Fe", 3 cent stamp (1960)
- Willa Cather, 8-cent stamp (1974)
- Georgia O'Keeffe, 32 cent stamp (1996)
- Georgia O'Keeffe, forever stamp (2013)
- Evangelo Klonis, 37 cent stamp (2002) (He started Evangelo's here in Santa Fe)

Some of the 1959 criteria used for the recommendations on commemorative stamps made by CSAC (Citizens Stamp Advisory Committee) to the PMG (Post Master General) include:

1. No living person shall be honored by portrayal on any United States postage
2. No living person shall be honored by portrayal on any United States postage stamp;
3. No American citizen may be honored by a United States commemorative postage stamp until at least 25 years after death;
4. Commemorative postage stamps honoring individuals will preferably be issued on the anniversaries of their births; and,
5. Events having widespread national appeal and significance may receive consideration for issuance of commemorative postage stamps;

US Coin Related to Santa Fe

Nina Otero-Warren is one of only four women honored by the US Mint on a quarter. She was the first female superintendent of Santa Fe Public Schools and an activist for women's right to vote. The 'tails' side of the coin features an image of Nina Otero-Warren on the left, and on the right are three individual Yucca flowers, the New Mexico state flower. It also has VOTO PARA LA MUJER, Spanish for the slogan "Votes for Women." (1922)

Awards, Kudos, Accolades, Superlatives, & Honors

American Express Travel: Santa Fe was chosen as one of the "2024 Trending

Destinations: Off the Beaten Path"

Best Life: Santa Fe was ranked #5 city among the "12 Best US Cities Every Traveler Should See"

Conde Nast Traveler: Santa Fe was ranked #2 in "The Best Places to Go in 2024"

Conde Nast Traveler: Santa Fe was ranked 2023 #6 "The 10 Friendliest Cities in the US"

Conde Nast Traveler: Santa Fe was ranked 2023 #2 " The Best Small Cities in the US"

Conde Nast Traveler: Bishop's Lodge was ranked #1 in 2023 "Top 20 Resorts in the Mountain West and #10 "Best Resorts of the World"

Conde Nast Traveler: Inn of the Five Graces was ranked #6 among "Top 10 Hotels in the Southwest & West" in 2023

Conde Nast Traveler UK: Santa Fe was chosen as one of the "Top 10 Destinations for Spring 2023"

Cosmopolitan: Santa Fe was ranked #2 destination among "40 of the Best Girls' Trip Destinations in the US to Book RTF Now"

Fodor's Travel: Bishop's Lodge was selected as one of the "Best Hotels in North America"

Food & Wine: Food & Wine Magazine Global Tastemaker Awards on the list of **"The 10 Best Cities for Neighborhood Restaurants in the U.S."**

Forbes Travel Guide: 2024 Forbes Travel Guide Star Award Winners: Bishop's Lodge, Four Seasons Resort Rancho Encantado Santa Fe, Geronimo, The Inn of the Five Graces, and Rosewood Inn of the Anasazi

Frommer's: Santa Fe was chosen as one of "Frommer's Best Places to Go in 2024"

Good Housekeeping: Santa Fe was chosen as a "Must-See" city in "the 2024 Best Family Travel Awards

Good Housekeeping: Santa Fe was selected as one of the "Best Solo Travel Destinations in the United States for an Unforgettable Adventure"

Lonely Planet: Santa Fe was chosen as one of "The Top 12 Places to Visit in the USA"

Men's Journal: Santa Fe was selected as one of the "9 Best Small Towns in America for Every Type of Traveler" and designated as the "Best for Art Lovers"

Moviemaker Magazine: Santa Fe was ranked #1 Smaller City in "Best Places to Live and Work as a MovieMaker"

Redbook Magazine: Santa Fe was ranked as #4 "Most Beautiful City in the World"

Retirebetternow.com Santa Fe was included among the "23 Best Places to Retire in the US in 2023."

Sunset Magazine: Santa Fe County was designated "Best US Western Destination in 2023"

Sunset Magazine: Bishop's Lodge named Winner, "Best Luxury Resorts 2023"

The Family Vacation Guide: Santa Fe was ranked #2 among "US Cultural Hotspots: The Top US Cities for a Vacation Packed With Culture"

Travel Awaits: Santa Fe was ranked #1 among "Most Beautiful US Train Trip to Experience in 2023"

Travel + Leisure Santa Fe was ranked #13 25 "Best Christmas Towns in the USA"

Travel + Leisure Santa Fe was ranked # 2 city in "15 Favorite Cities in the United States 2023"

Travel + Leisure Santa Fe was ranked # 21 of "25 Favorite Cities in the World 2023"

Travel + Leisure Santa Fe was chosen as one of "The 21 Best US Cities for Fall Travel"

Travel + Leisure Bishops Lodge and Rosewood Inn of the Anasazi were chosen as two of "The 500 Best Hotels in the World"

TripAdvisor Sazon was ranked #6, Geronimo was ranked #11, and Sassella was ranked #13 among "Best Fine Dining Restaurants – United States"

USA Today 10 Best: La Fonda on the Plaza was ranked #9 "Best Historic Hotel 2023"

USA Today 10 Best: Santa Fe Wine & Chile Fiesta was ranked #7 "Best Wine Festival 2023"

USA Today 10 Best: IAIA Museum of Contemporary Native Art was ranked #3 and Museum of International Folk Art ranked #10 "Best Art Museum 2023"

USA Today 10 Best: Santa Fe Plaza was ranked #6 "Best Public Square 2023"

USA Today 10 Best: Santa Fe Spirits was ranked #2 "Best Craft Brandy 2023"

Wall Street Journal: The Santa Fe Ski Basin was ranked #89 among "The 100 Best Ski Resorts in the US and Canada"

Wine Spectator: Santa Fe was included in "10 Great Destinations for Food and Wine Across America"

World's Best Cities Santa Fe was ranked 3rd among "America's Best Small Cities." www.worldsbestcities.com/rankings/americas-best-small-cities/

Chapter 17

THE BUSINESS
OF
SANTA FE

Santa Fe Is Not Completely About Tourism

Santa Fe's economy *is* based largely on tourism with an average of 1.6 million visitors each year who spend more than $1 billion annually.

Not surprisingly, as the capital of New Mexico, the government is the largest employer. However, scientific research has become significant since Santa Fe is only 45 miles from Los Alamos National Laboratory (LANL). LANL is one of the largest research laboratories in the country working on defense-related projects, conducting research on technology associated with nuclear weapons and deterrence, energy production, and health, safety, and environmental concerns.

Over one-third of LANL's employees live in Santa Fe, and several new research-related firms and high-technology spinoff companies are in Santa Fe. Santa Fe is becoming a regional medical center, with St. Vincent Regional Medical Center serving seven counties and one of the city's largest employers. Albuquerque-based Presbyterian Hospital has moved into the market to serve Santa Fe's growing population. Some local companies manufacture electronic instruments and textiles.

Data USA 2021 (datausa.io)

The largest industries in Santa Fe are Health Care and Social Assistance, Retail Trade, and Professional, Scientific, and Technical Services. The highest-paying industries are Professional, Scientific, and Technical Services ($71,916), Finance and Insurance ($65,152), and Utilities ($60,221).

The most common job groups, by the number of people living in Santa Fe: Management, Office & Administrative Support, and Sales & Related.

The industries with the best median earnings for men in 2021 are Professional, Scientific, & Management, & Administrative & Waste Management Services ($64,348), Finance & Insurance, & Real Estate & Rental & Leasing ($62,955), and Public Administration ($51,480).

The industries with the best median earnings for women in 2021 are Professional, Scientific, & Management, & Administrative & Waste Management Services ($48,810), Finance & Insurance, & Real Estate & Rental & Leasing ($48,547), and Public Administration ($48,370).

The median household income in Santa Fe in 2021 grew to $61,990 from the previous year's $57,274

Significant Job Categories in Santa Fe

- **Healthcare** includes private medical practices, clinics, and healthcare facilities

- **Hospitality and Tourism** include hotels, resorts, restaurants, and tour companies.

- **Real Estate Development and Management** includes real estate development, property management, and construction.

- **Retail and Art Galleries** include art galleries, boutiques, and specialty shops

- **Professional Services** include law firms, accounting firms, consulting firms, and others.

Largest Employers in Santa Fe in 2023

Public (per New Mexico Partnership in 2023)

1. State of New Mexico: 3,250
2. Santa Fe Public Schools 1,800
3. City of Santa Fe 1,400
4. Federal Government +/-1,000
5. Santa Fe Opera 750
6. Santa Fe Community College 717
7. New Mexico Department of Cultural Affairs 520
8. New Mexico House of Representatives 350
9. New Mexico School for the Deaf 350
10. Los Alamos National Laboratory
11. Santa Fe County 850
12. Santa Fe Indian School (200)
13. Institute of American Indian Arts (200)

Private (per New Mexico Partnership)

1. Albertsons
2. Camel Rock Casino
3. Christus St. Vincent Regional Medical Center
4. Hilton Buffalo Thunder Resort & Casino
5. Meow Wolf

6. Peters Corporation
7. Presbyterian Medical Services
8. Santa Fe New Mexican
9. Santa Fe Properties
10. Santa Maria el Mirador
11. Ski Santa Fe (seasonal)
12. The Santa Fe Opera
13. Thermo BioAnalysis
14. Wal-Mart
15. Whole Foods Market

Santa Fe's Significant Job Providers

- State of New Mexico
- Santa Fe School District
- U.S. Government
- City of Santa Fe
- St. Vincent Hospital
- Santa Fe Opera
- Santa Fe Community College
- College of Santa Fe
- Presbyterian Medical Services
- County of Santa Fe
- Cities of Gold Casino
- Camel Rock Casino
- Thornburg Companies
- DeVargas Center
- First National Bank of Santa Fe
- Iron Stone Bank
- Rio Grande Title companies
- Santa Fe Art Institute
- Strategic Analytics

Santa Fe Area's Largest Employers (Albuquerque Business First 2023)

- Christus St. Vincent 2,485
- Presbyterian Santa Fe Medical Center 579
- Santa Fe Community College 535
- St. John's College 170
- Toyota of Santa Fe 145

Zippia's Best Companies to Work For

(Zippia score uses salary, financial health, and employee diversity)

1. Descartes Labs (4.5)
2. Santa Fe Public Schools (4.5)
3. Santa Fe Institute (4.5)
4. Toyota of Santa Fe (4.2)
5. Thermo BioAnalysis 4.2

Glass Door's 2023 Best Companies to Work For in Santa Fe

(5.0 highest; minimum 10 reviews)

- 5.0 Pachama
- 4.9 Ironside Human Resources
- 4.9 Continued
- 4.8 Host Healthcare
- 4.8 Menu Pros
- 4.8 Alloy
- 4.7 Techsource
- 4.7 National Water Services
- 4.7 Crumbacher Business Systems
- 4.7 Virtú Investments
- 4.6 Heal.me
- 4.6 Santa Fe College

- 4.6 United Global Technologies
- 4.6 Navarro Research & Engineering
- 4.6 ROI Healthcare Solutions
- 4.6 The VA Group
- 4.6 WildEarth Guardians
- 4.6 Enterprise Bank & Trust
- 4.5 Umbrella Corporation
- 4.5 Descartes Labs
- 4.5 Santa Fe Opera
- 4.5 New Mexico Consortium
- 4.5 DVR Softek
- 4.5 Global Resources
- 4.5 SHC
- 4.5 Merrell
- 4.5 Epic Consulting Group

Companies with Headquarters in Santa Fe

- **Avalon Trust** manages over one billion dollars in assets for clients around the world
- **BiosGroup** is a spin-off from the Santa Fe Institute.
- **Cottonwood Technology Fund** is a venture capital fund
- **Deep Web Technologies** is a software company that specializes in mining the Deep Web, which is the part of the Internet that is not directly searchable.
- **Figaro Systems** provides seatback and wireless titling software installations to opera houses and other music performance venues worldwide. It was the first company to provide assistive technology that enables individualized, simultaneous, multi-lingual dialogue and libretto-reading for audiences
- **Flow Science, Inc.** is a developer of computational fluid dynamics software
- **Meow Wolf** was founded in 2008 as an immersive, experiential, and

location-based entertainment venue. By 2022, the company had grown to 980 employees, with a revenue of $158 million with locations in Santa Fe, Denver, Las Vegas, Grapevine, Texas, with Houston next.

- **OpenEye Scientific Software** is an American software company founded in 1997. It develops large-scale molecular modeling applications and toolkits.

- **Santa Fe Brewing Company** was established in 1988 as New Mexico's first craft brewery and has since become the state's largest brewery.

- **Solstar Space** provides WiFi Access Points for Lunar Orbit. In 2022 *Solstar* began the development of WiFi Access Points for future lunar orbit *space* stations.

- **Thornburg Investment Management, Inc.** is a private, independent investment management company with assets of over $46 billion under management and advisement as of January 2020.

Gone, But Not Forgotten

- **Palace Grocery.** It opened as a grocery store in 1959 on Palace Avenue but was later changed into a convenience store, then a private office and gallery.

- **Jake Gold's Old Curiosity Shop (Gold's Free Museum)** was located at the corner of West San Francisco Street and Burro Alley. It was the first Indian curio business in Santa Fe and was open from 1862 until 1905.

Business Support

The Santa Fe Business Incubator provides a variety of assistance to new companies.

The Small Business Development Center is available to assist entrepreneurs.

SCORE provides mentoring to business owners offering free and low-cost business workshops to help small business owners and entrepreneurs gain the skills they need.

www.ingramcontent.com/pod-product-compliance
Lightning Source LLC
Chambersburg PA
CBHW071153130626
46553CB00004B/1646